Quick & Easy Guide to
SEWING TECHNIQUES

Quick & Easy Guide to SEWING TECHNIQUES

Butterick Publishing

Editor: Mary Anne Symons Brown
Writers: Sandra Lenker
            Amy Sue Addison Licameli
Technical Illustrator: Marcy Altimano
Fashion Illustrator: Susan Blackman Bevil
Cover Design: Winnie Young
Cover Photography: Peter Polymenakos

Copyright © 1978
Butterick Publishing
708 Third Avenue
New York, New York 10017

A Division of American Can Company

Library of Congress Catalog Card Number:
77-93795
International Standard Book Number:
0-88421-081-2

First Printing, April 1978
Second Printing, July 1978

Printed in the U.S.A.

contents

sewing is something special...

Sewing is one of the most interesting, creative skills you can learn. It allows you to make clothes, accessories or items for your home to suit your very own taste for fashion, comfort and convenience. Best of all, sewing is fun.

This book of *Quick and Easy Sewing Techniques* is planned just for you. It sums up all the clever ideas of designers and professional experts so you can use the sewing methods that work fine, every time.

Whether you have sewn before or are just beginning, you'll find plenty of hints that will help you make handsome, custom-finished projects.

What will you find inside *Quick and Easy Sewing Techniques?* Here's an overview.

The first section is Sewing Basics, pages 10-17. It reviews the details about patterns, marking, basting, pressing and fusing. Read it first to be certain you know the latest techniques as you start sewing.

Next, in alphabetical order, are sections which explain the special sewing skills you'll need to complete a garment or other project. In them you'll be able to follow the step-by-step directions and illustrations, from start to finish. Since the sections are arranged alphabetically, you'll be able to locate the facts you need quickly and conveniently.

In addition, there are many cross-references in each section. If you're attaching a band, you'll also learn to refer to Interfacing, Marking or other special sections which relate to the job you're doing at the moment.

There's also an index at the end of the book which includes all the words or phrases you're likely to come across as you read pattern catalogs, guidesheets or sections in *Quick and Easy Sewing Techniques.*

Once you have mastered the skills in the Sewing Basics and alphabetical sections from Bands to Zippers, read the final section, Careers That Build on Sewing Skills, page 157. It's full of facts about job opportunities that will allow you to put your talents to work.

You might be surprised to learn how many people have jobs which depend on their understanding of sewing. Perhaps there's a position that's just right for you...as an artist or author, editor or educator, salesperson or sewing machine operator or mechanic. Whatever your career goals or personal skills, there are employment opportunities worth looking into.

The whole idea behind *Quick and Easy Sewing Techniques* is that sewing is simple and useful in many, many situations. We hope it will help you see for yourself that sewing *is* something special.

Quick & Easy Guide to
SEWING TECHNIQUES

sewing basics

There are many sewing aids and techniques which can help you complete a garment or other project easily and efficiently.

In this section you'll learn general information about understanding a pattern, marking, basting, pressing and fusing. Once you understand the importance of each step, you'll be ready to start sewing interesting, exciting fashions, accessories or decorative items.

understanding a pattern

A pattern is a guide which gives you the step-by-step information you need to complete a successful project.

It's a good idea to read every word on the pattern envelope, guidesheet and tissue sections before you begin.

On the front of a pattern envelope, you'll find a photograph or illustration of the finished item, the size, style and special hints about the project, such as "For Knits Only" or "Dual Size Pattern, sizes 6 and 8 included."

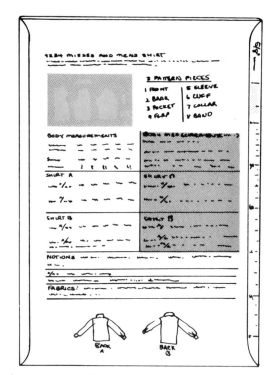

On the back of the pattern envelope, the fabric requirements are explained, in yards and meters. In addition, there are illustrations of the backview or special construction details, advice about the suitability of plaids or other fabrics, standard body measurements if the pattern is for a garment, a sketch of the pattern pieces, a listing of suggested fabrics and required notions as well as a general description of the project, such as "Pants with drawstring or elastic waistband."

In fact, the information on the back of the pattern envelope can be used to develop a shopping list for the supplies you'll need to complete your project.

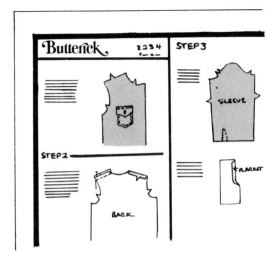

Inside the envelope is the pattern guidesheet, which gives thorough information about the skills and techniques required.

On the guidesheet you will find directions for laying out your fabric correctly and placing pattern pieces on it. The guidesheet also includes exact directions for cutting, marking and sewing.

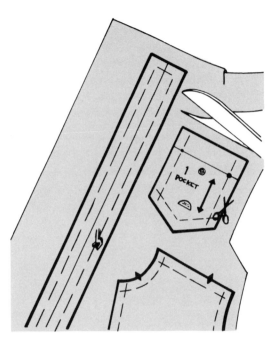

The actual pattern pieces are printed on tissue paper and must be cut apart so you can place them on your fabric correctly.

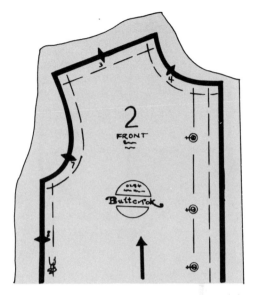

Each pattern piece has a solid line around the edge, indicating where to cut. It may also have notches along the edge.

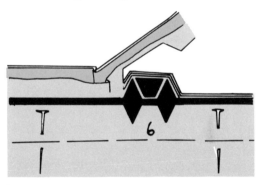

When cutting out a piece with notches, cut *around* them. These notches are numbered and will help you match up the various pieces as you put the item together.

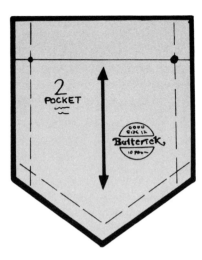

Looking closely at a pattern piece, you'll notice a grainline printed on it. This describes how the piece should be placed—either on the lengthwise, crosswise or True Bias of the fabric. For more information about fabric grain, see page 30.

The pattern piece will also note whether to place it on a fold or a double thickness of fabric.

The seamline is indicated by a broken line, ⅝″ (15 mm) inside the cutting line.

The piece may also have other markings to indicate where to sew darts, tucks, pockets and similar details used for shaping or decorating an item.

laying out a pattern

The best advice about placing the pattern pieces on your fabric can be found on the pattern guidesheet.

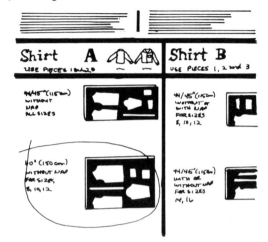

Circle the layout which describes the type and width of your fabric.

Fold the fabric, if necessary, as the guidesheet suggests.

Place the pattern pieces on the fabric according to the sketch.

Be careful to place the pieces which are to be on a fold, exactly as illustrated.

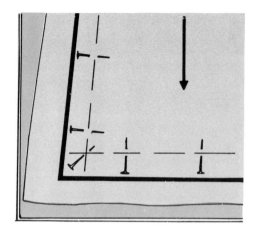

Pin the pattern pieces to the fabric.

■ The pins should be perpendicular to the cutting line, with the heads resting next to it. To keep the corners in place while cutting, place pins on the diagonal.

Cut out the item, using sharp scissors and long, even strokes.

marking

Marking is a technique for transferring the lines or other indications on the pattern tissue to your fabric.

Marking is necessary to enable you to sew darts, pockets or other design details accurately.

All of the pattern symbols which describe how and where fabric sections are shaped or joined should be marked on the fabric—*after* cutting but *before* the pattern tissue is removed.

TAILOR'S WAX

Tailor's wax is available in the same forms as tailor's chalk. It can be used for marking most types of fabric. Generally it leaves a somewhat more durable marking than chalk and will not brush off as you are working on the item.

One word of caution—always test a fabric before using tailor's wax. As a rule, the markings disappear completely after pressing but on some fabrics tailor's wax leaves a permanent spot.

Once you have decided that tailor's wax is suitable for your fabric, transfer markings with it in the same way as with tailor's chalk.

TRACING PAPER AND WHEEL

Tracing paper and a tracing wheel are used to mark plain-colored fabrics and certain prints which are firmly woven or knitted.

It is a very fast, accurate method for most fabrics but it is not suitable for loopy, extra thick or furry fabrics or sheer ones on which markings may show through on the right side.

Always consider the markings from tracing paper as permanent. Some types of tracing paper are designed so that the markings will wash out when the fabric is laundered but, even so, there may be slight markings left.

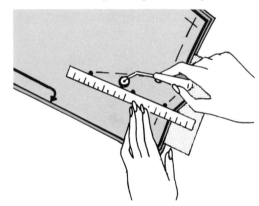

Place single-faced tracing paper on the wrong side of the fabric.

- To mark two layers of fabric at the same time place double-faced tracing paper between them, on the wrong side.

Use heavy cardboard or a similar heavy, stiff backing under the tracing paper so the markings will be sharp and clear.

Roll a smooth or serrated tracing wheel along a straight-edged ruler to transfer markings. Use an "X" to indicate dots, squares or other small pattern markings.

TAILOR'S CHALK

Tailor's chalk is available as a pencil or a small rectangle. Both types work equally well. The markings made by tailor's chalk can be easily brushed off any fabric.

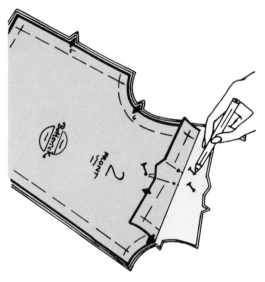

Push a pin through each dot, triangle or other pattern symbol you want to transfer.

- Be certain that the pin passes through both layers of fabric if you are marking two layers at one time.

Remove the pattern tissue, forcing the pin heads through the paper as you do so.

Make a chalk dot on the wrong side of each fabric layer at each pin.

TAILOR'S TACKS

Tailor's tacks are thread markings. They take more time and effort than other marking methods but are very useful for certain fabrics, especially sheers or delicate, spongy or multicolored fabrics which cannot be clearly marked by other techniques.

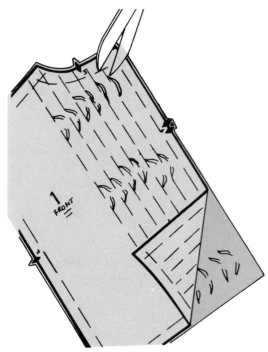

Use a double strand of light-colored thread.

Sew a large loop over the mark you want to transfer.

Cut through the loop.

Remove the pattern tissue.

- If the tailor's tack is being used to mark two layers of fabric, pull the layers apart gently and clip the thread between them to leave short lengths in each layer.

basting

Basting is a temporary method used to hold fabric in place until you have completed your permanent stitching. It allows you to check the fit or accuracy of a seam or other area.

There are several basting techniques: Pin Basting, Hand Basting and Machine Basting.

PIN BASTING

This is a fast and easy way to baste areas where a minimum amount of control is needed.

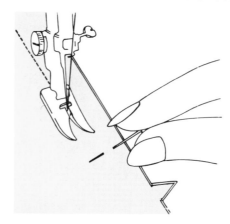

Match pattern markings such as notches or darts, then place pins at right angles to the seamline.

Remove the pins as you stitch.

- Sewing over pins is harmful to your machine and your needles.

HAND BASTING

This is an excellent basting method for hard-to-handle fabrics such as velvets or fine silks. It is also useful for areas where extra control is needed, such as tricky corners and curves.

For more information about this technique, refer to Hand Sewing, page 77. Here are the general hand-basting steps.

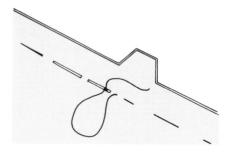

Match pattern markings and pin baste the garment sections together.

Secure your thread to the fabric.

Take long, uneven stitches about 1″ (25 mm) apart and ½″ (13 mm) long.

- You can take several stitches at one time to complete basting quickly.

- For areas where you need a little more control, take short ½″ (13 mm) stitches about ½″ (13 mm) apart.

MACHINE BASTING

Machine basting uses a long machine stitch. It is used mainly as a quick way of joining seams to check fit or accuracy. Because the stitches are long, they are easy to remove and any adjustments can be made simply.

Before you machine baste, test your fabric to be certain that the sewing machine needle does not leave permanent marks. If it does, basting must be done inside the seam allowance, not on the seamline.

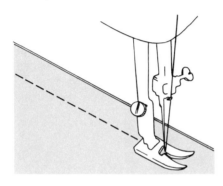

Set your machine stitch to its longest length.

■ It is usually 6 stitches per inch (a stitch length of 2.5 mm).

Match pattern markings and pin baste.

Stitch the sections of fabric together with the long machine stitch.

Check the fit or accuracy of the item and make any necessary adjustments before you stitch the seam permanently.

Remove the basting stitches *as soon as* you have completed your permanent stitching.

■ This prevents the machine basting from being caught in seams that cross and keeps it from interfering as you press.

pressing

Good pressing techniques are as necessary to well-made garments as expert sewing skills. Pressing and sewing work together to help you achieve professional results.

Pressing is the process of lifting and lowering the iron. The combination of heat, pressure and steam allows you to mold, shape and smooth your garment as you sew. With good pressing habits, you'll be able to make beautiful garments.

Your pressing equipment should be near your sewing machine since it is important to press at all stages of sewing. You will need an ironing table and a good steam iron, a presscloth and either a press mitt or tailor's ham. Other pieces of pressing equipment can make the job a bit easier, but are not necessary.

The following hints will help you develop successful pressing techniques.

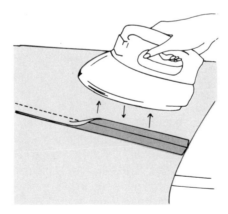

1. Pressing should not be confused with ironing. In pressing, the iron is lifted and then lowered onto the garment rather than pushed over it as in ironing.

2. Press from the wrong side of the fabric whenever possible. That way all seams can be seen clearly and pressed correctly.

3. Sometimes you can't press on the wrong side because the seams or garment sections are enclosed, such as with a patch pocket. In this case, use a press cloth when you are working from the right side to prevent overpressing or causing a shiny mark on the fabric. A piece of lightweight fabric such as batiste, organdy or cheesecloth works well. An excellent choice for fabrics with a nap, such as velveteen or corduroy, is a piece of the same fabric. The two naps should be placed face to face to prevent the nap from becoming crushed. This technique also helps avoid press marks on your fabric.

4. Never press over pins because they will leave an impression on your fabric and scratch your iron.

5. Be cautious when pressing over basting—it can also leave marks on your fabric. Always use white or light-colored thread for basting because the steam may release the dye from the thread which will mark your fabric.

6. Use the correct heat setting for your fabric. First test a scrap of fabric. If it seems to stick, melt, pucker or create smoke, the iron is much too hot. Synthetic fibers tend to be quite sensitive to heat, so set the iron on "cool" or "warm" if necessary.

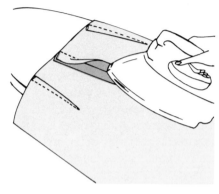

7. Always press seams and darts before other seams are stitched across them. This helps reduce bulk and prevents a lumpy appearance in the finished garment.

8. Check the fit of the garment before you press any sharp creases such as pleats.

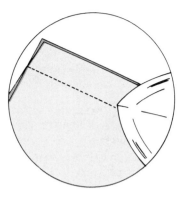

9. Always press seams flat first, before you press them open. This allows the stitches to settle into the fabric before the seam is pressed open. It's a good way to eliminate puckers on seams which do not appear flat.

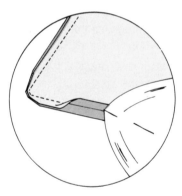

10. Enclosed seams, such as those on collars and lapels, should also be pressed flat first, then pressed open before the garment section is turned right side out. Careful pressing in this way allows the seams to fall sharply along the edge of the finished garment. Press enclosed seams with the tip of your iron or use a point presser to get to the hard-to-reach areas.

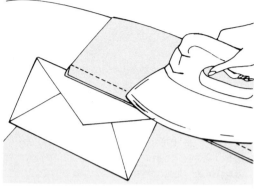

11. Use the tip of your iron to press only the seam allowances if the fabric is likely to show pressing marks on the right side of the garment. Place a piece of white paper—an envelope or a sheet of stationery—under the seam allowances as you press to avoid pressing an indentation into the outer fabric.

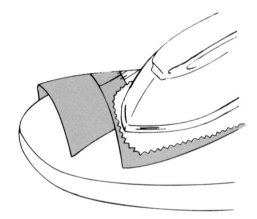

12. Press curved seams and darts over a curved surface such as a pressing mitt or tailor's ham.

fusing

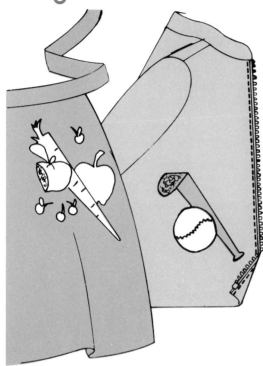

Anyone who is interested in sewing is eager to learn about new products which make sewing easier, more efficient and even more creative.

Fusible products do just that. These sewing aids can be pressed into position to attach facings, hold hems or add decorative details.

Fusibles are available in two different products: fusible interfacings and fusible web.

FUSIBLE INTERFACING

Fusible interfacings are woven or nonwoven fabrics which have a heat-sensitive bonding agent on one side. As the fabric is pressed, the bonding agent melts and attaches the interfacing to your garment. This saves stitching time and provides a handsome, smooth interfacing. For more information about fusible interfacings and how to use them, see Interfacing, page 87.

FUSIBLE WEB

Fusible web has a similar bonding agent but is a thin veil-like net which is used to join two layers of fabric together. It can be used to apply trims or appliqués, for hemming and many other sewing techniques. For convenience, fusible web is sold in thin strips ½" (13 mm) or 1" (25 mm) wide or in wider pieces available by the yard or meter.

Just as with any sewing product, follow the manufacturer's directions for working with fusibles. These general guidelines will help you use fusibles efficiently.

1. Do all your preliminary pressing first, then place the fusible where you want to attach it to the fabric.

2. Steam and heat are the most important factors in fusing successfully. A wet presscloth is essential with most fusible interfacings or webs to insure a permanent bond.

3. Fusible products can be used on most fabrics that can be steam pressed, except some sheers or synthetics, such as vinyl, which can't withstand high heat. Following the package directions, always test the fusible on a small scrap of fabric before using it on a garment or other item.

4. Do not allow the bonding agent of the interfacing or the fusible web to touch your iron. It will melt and stick to it and is, at best, very difficult to remove.

Fusing is intended to be a permanent process, so plan carefully before you attach a fusible interfacing or web to your garment.

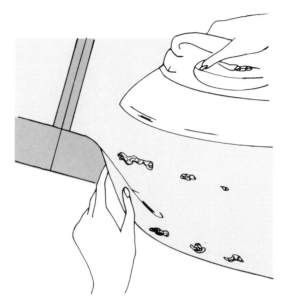

However, fusible web can be removed if you want to lower a hem or correct a mistake in attaching trim. Simply apply heat and steam to the bonded area and pull the two layers of fabric apart while they are still warm. Remove the excess residue of the web by placing a scrap of fabric over it, pressing and removing it while the area is still warm. Repeat this process until most of the residue is removed. Don't expect to be able to remove all of the web residue. A small amount will probably remain on the fabric. In the few cases that this causes problems, you might be able to remove the remaining residue with rubbing alcohol. Be careful to test your fabric first to be certain the alcohol won't damage it.

bands

Bands are decorative accents which add detail, contrast and fashion interest.

Extended Bands, Placket Bands and Knit Bands are the three basic types. They may be used alone or in combination on a garment.

Exact directions for attaching bands depend on the design of the garment and the placement of the bands. Rely on your pattern guidesheet for specific instructions.

extended bands

Extended bands are just that—extended parts of the garment that become a design feature. They may look like facings but they aren't, and the method used to attach them is quite different. Extended bands are often used at necklines or armholes.

These bands are easy to make if you follow these general steps.

Interface the band if necessary.

■ Refer to Interfacing, page 86, for more information.

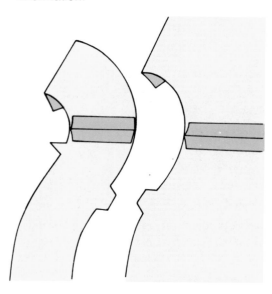

Pin the band to the garment, right sides together, carefully matching the notches on the band to the notches on the garment.

■ It may be helpful to look closely at your pattern tissue first to see how each section joins the other.

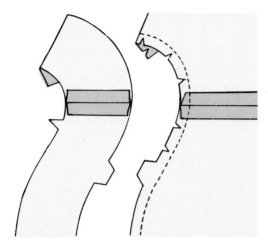

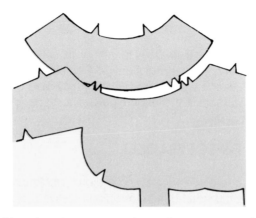

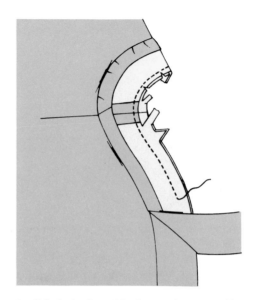

■ On curved areas, staystitch and clip the seam allowance of the inside or smaller curved edge of the garment. The seam allowances will then spread to match the seamline of the band evenly.

Since bands are extensions of a garment and not facings, they need to be faced. Some bands are designed to fold back on themselves to form a facing. Other bands are faced using a separate fabric piece which is identical to the shape of the band.

2. Stitch the band facing to the band, if your band has a separate facing piece.

3. Grade the seam allowances and clip or notch where necessary.

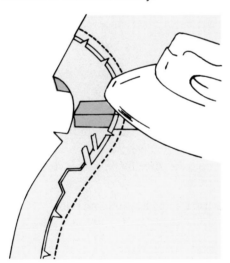

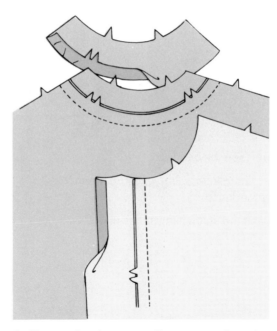

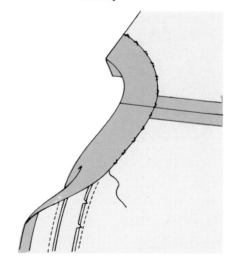

Stitch the band to the garment.

Grade the seam allowances and clip any curved areas.

Press the seam allowances toward the band.

1. Turn under the seam allowance at the edge of the band facing and press.

4. Turn the facing to the wrong side and slipstitch the edge which has been pressed under to the garment along the seamline.

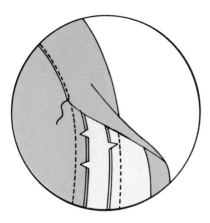

Some bands are finished by machine from the right side.

1. Stitch the right side of the band to the wrong side of the garment.

2. Then flip the band over the raw edge of the garment.

3. Turn under the raw edge of the band itself and edgestitch the band from the right side of the garment to attach it.

placket bands

Placket bands are used for openings, most often at necklines and sleeves. Complete instructions are included in your guidesheet. Follow them to the letter to put a placket band in its place.

ONE-PIECE PLACKET

The one-piece placket is completed with these plain and simple steps that eliminate the problem of tricky corners.

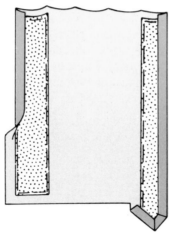

Interface the band.

■ Refer to Interfacing, page 86, for more information.

Press the seam allowances under.

Transfer the markings from the pattern tissue to the wrong side of the band sections. Use tracing paper, dressmaker's chalk or another suitable method.

■ Check the details on Marking, page 13, to choose a suitable technique. Accuracy in marking is the clue to certain success.

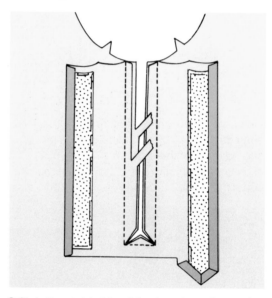

Stitch the right side of the band section to the wrong side of the garment following the stitching lines.

Slash between the stitching lines and clip into the corners.

Grade the seams to eliminate bulk.

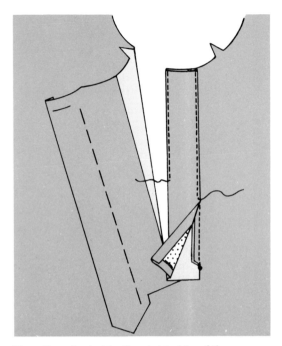

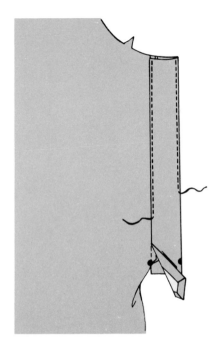

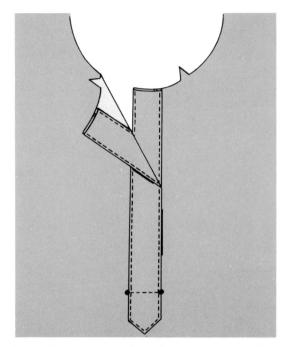

Turn the placket to the right side of the garment.

Press the placket on the foldlines indicated.

Edgestitch the placket underlap, keeping the overlap free.

Edgestitch the two long sides of the placket overlap, keeping the underlap free.

Place the two placket sections one on top of the other.

Topstitch the bottom of the placket, as indicated on your pattern piece, to secure the overlap to the underlap.

TWO-PIECE PLACKET

The two-piece placket is used at curved areas or places where the inside of the band would be exposed. An open neckline is an ideal place for a two-piece placket.

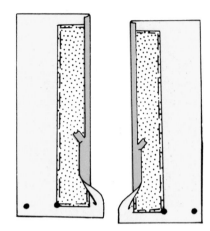

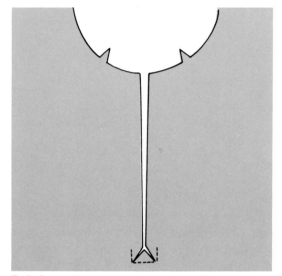

Reinforce the garment opening with small machine stitches, approximately 15-20 per inch (each 25 mm).

Slash the opening and clip into the corners.

Interface each placket band.

- Refer to Interfacing, page 86, for more information.

Transfer the markings from the pattern tissue to the wrong side of the band sections. Use tracing paper, dressmaker's chalk or another suitable method.

- Check the details on Marking, page 13, to choose a technique. Accuracy in marking is the clue to certain success.

Press under the long seam allowance on the uninterfaced side of each placket band.

Trim the seam allowance to ¼" (6 mm).

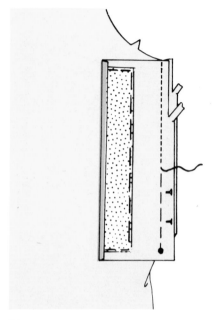

Pin baste this placket band which will form the underlap to the garment opening with the right side of the band next to the wrong side of the garment.

- In girls' or women's garments, the underlap is formed on the left side.

- In boys' or men's garments, the underlap is formed on the right side.

Stitch the band to the garment above the marking at the bottom of the band.

Grade the seam allowances.

Press the seam toward the band.

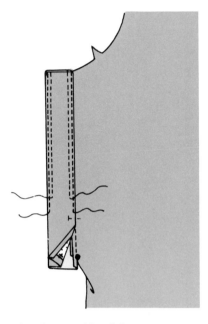

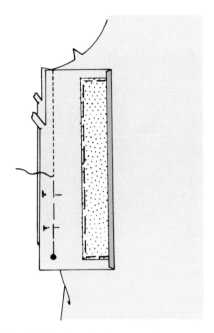

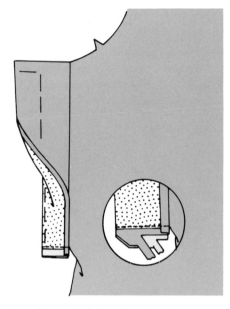

Turn the band to the outside of the garment.

Press the band on the foldline indicated on the pattern piece.

Pin the remaining edge of the band over the seam.

Edgestitch the two long edges of the band above the markings at the bottom of the band.

Topstitch ¼" (6 mm) from the edgestitching.

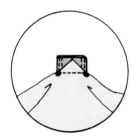

Stitch the bottom edge of the band to the lower end of the placket opening from the inside of the garment.

Pin baste the placket band which will form the overlap to the remaining side of the garment opening with the right side of the band next to the wrong side of the garment.

■ In girls' and women's garments, the overlap is formed on the right side.

■ In boys' and men's garments, the overlap is formed on the left side.

Stitch the band to the garment above the marking at the bottom of the band.

Grade the seam allowances.

Press the seam toward the band.

Fold the band in half, right sides together, along the foldline indicated on the pattern piece.

Stitch across the lower edge of the band.

Trim the seam allowance.

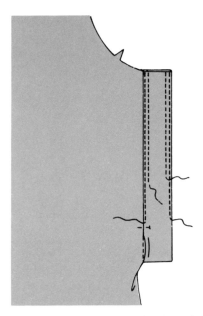

Turn the band to the right side of the garment.

Press the band on the foldline indicated on the pattern piece.

Pin the remaining edge of the band over the seam.

Edgestitch the two long edges of the band above the stitching line indicated on the pattern piece.

Topstitch ¼″ (6 mm) from the edgestitching.

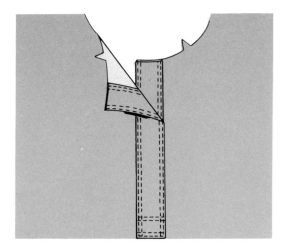

Place placket bands one on top of the other as they will be when the garment is worn.

Edgestitch close to the remaining edges of the overlap below the previous stitching.

- Stitch through all thicknesses of both bands.

- Match lines of stitching with previous stitching for a neat finish.

Topstitch ¼″ (6 mm) from the edgestitching.

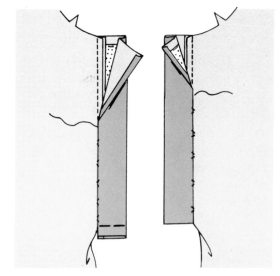

If you prefer, you can attach the band sections without edgestiching or topstitching. Follow the same basic steps described above *except* stitch the band sections to the garment with *right* sides of the fabric together, flip the band sections up and over the seam allowances to the wrong side of the garment, and slipstitch along the seamline from the inside.

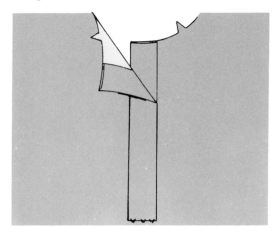

Slipstitch the bottom edge of the overlap in place.

knit bands

Bands made from knit fabric are ideal for finishing the edges of knit garments. These bands allow you to take advantage of the stretchability of a knit to give a professional look to an item.

A knit band is always cut a bit shorter than the edge to which it will be joined. As the band is stretched slightly and stitched to the garment, it helps stabilize the edge and shape it for a handsome appearance and comfortable fit.

The Bound Seam Method is the technique used to attach most knit bands.

BOUND SEAM METHOD

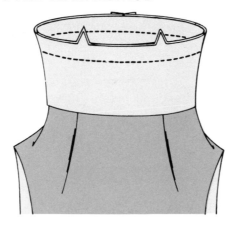

Stitch the band to the garment, right sides together, matching notches.

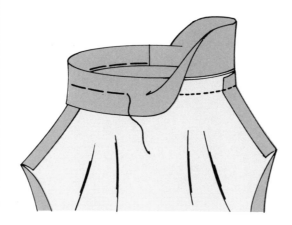

Press all seam allowances toward the band.

Fold the band back, over the seam allowances.

- It will extend beyond the seams on the inside of the garment.

Baste along the seamline through all thicknesses to hold the band in place.

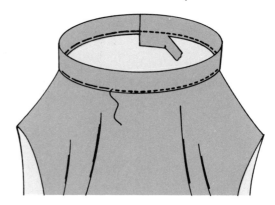

Edgestitch from the right side of the band through all layers or "stitch-in-the-ditch" by sewing in the ridge of the seam.

Trim the seam allowances of the band close to the row of edgestitching on the wrong side of the garment.

belts and belt carriers

Belts can be plain or fancy. Either way, they add a final touch of beauty and style.

Once you learn the basic techniques for making belts, you can use creativity to adapt your best ideas to make slim and stunning or high, wide and handsome ties, sashes or cummerbunds.

Why not make more than one belt? Each one will give you and your outfit a whole new fashion image.

Keep belts where they belong by attaching belt carriers made with the new no-turn method. It's the easiest idea ever.

BELTS

The best belts accent your waistline and add impact to your wardrobe. Use the same fabric as you did for your garment, or choose an interesting trim. Just follow these simple steps.

tie belts

There are two basic methods used to make tie belts. Fold and Stitch is a fast and foolproof way to create an easy tie. The technique is especially good for sturdy or heavy fabrics such as corduroy which may be hard to turn. The Stitch and Turn Method is more suitable for slinky fabrics such as jersey which are difficult to press.

FOLD AND STITCH METHOD

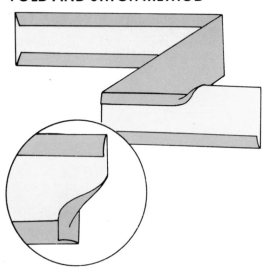

Press all the edges toward the wrong side.

- Be sure to fold accurately along the seamlines.

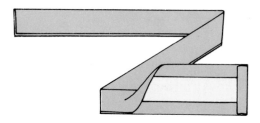

Fold the belt in half lengthwise, wrong sides together, matching the edges.

- Thick and bulky corners can be slimmed down by mitering. Fold and press the corner diagonally where the seamlines cross. Trim away most, but not all, of the corner, and miter by refolding along the seamlines so the edges meet without overlapping.

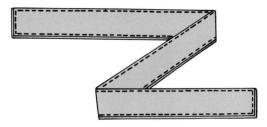

Edgestitch through all layers all around.

- If the belt starts to twist or ripple as you stitch, hold it firmly, with one hand behind the presser foot and one in front, while allowing the machine to feed the fabric through it.

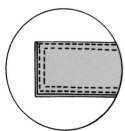

- For a sporty look, add another row of stitching about ¼″ (6 mm) inside the first row.

STITCH AND TURN METHOD

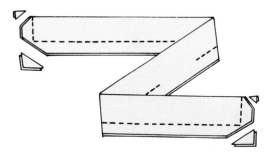

Fold the fabric strip lengthwise, right sides together.

Stitch a seam along all three cut edges, leaving a 3-4″ (7.5-10 cm) opening in the center of the long side for turning.

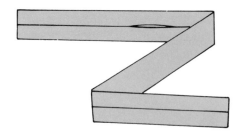

- If your fabric is heavy, first stitch the long side, leaving a 3-4″ (7.5-10 cm) opening for turning. Then center the seam and sew the ends.

Trim the seam allowances at the ends. Miter corners, as necessary, to remove excess bulk.

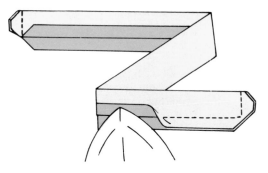

Press the seams open with the point of your iron.

Turn the belt right side out by pushing it through the opening with a ruler or long wooden spoon handle.

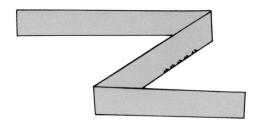

Slipstitch the opening so the stitches are flat and not obvious. This allows the belt edges to lie flat.

easy fun belts

Almost anything can be used to make an interesting belt. Try ribbon, drapery tie cording, fake fur, leather or vinyl, braid or woven trims. Let your imagination be your guide.

Some of the most exciting belts begin with the inspiration of a unique buckle or button. Shop around—you'll find good ideas at every turn in a fabric, decorating or home furnishings store.

Pick up some cording that will complement your garment. Or, cover your own cord (see Bias, page 34) to make a corded belt. Try mixing colors or thicknesses, or both! Braid them, macramé them or just mix and twist. Add a few wood or ceramic beads and you've created a great fashion belt.

Flat trims make fashion-right belts in a flash. Cut the trim long enough to wrap around your waist and tie with some extra length for the hanging ends. Simply fringe the ends or just turn them under and stitch. If you prefer, add a buckle as a closing fashion statement.

To buckle up your belt, choose one of the many buckle types, including rings, which are available in any notions department.

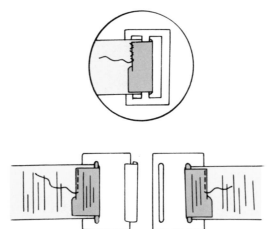

Slip the belt through the buckle and stitch securely by hand or machine.

■ Use the zipper foot attachment on your sewing machine to stitch as closely as possible to the buckle as you attach it to the belt.

BELT CARRIERS

Belt carriers are fabric or thread loops which are sewn onto a garment to hold the belt in place.

fabric belt carriers

Using the same fabric as you did for the garment, prepare a narrow strip long enough to be cut apart to form as many belt carriers as necessary.

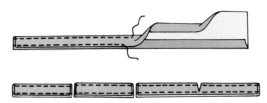

Begin with a fabric strip twice as wide as your completed carrier.

Cut this strip to a length which measures as long as all the carriers combined plus seam allowances for each carrier.

■ For example, if you need two belt carriers of 1½" (38 mm), cut a strip 3" (75 mm) *plus* 2½" (65 mm) for a total length of 5½" (140 mm), allowing seam allowances of ⅝" (15 mm) on each end of the two carriers.

Complete the carrier strip following the instructions for a Fold and Stitch Belt, page 26.

■ There is no need to finish the ends because they will be enclosed inside the garment when the carriers are attached.

To help reduce bulk in a belt carrier, use fusible web.

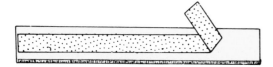

Cut a fabric strip along the selvage edge.

- Be certain the strip is the exact width and length you will need to prepare all the belt carriers your garment requires. Refer to the measuring directions given above.

Cut a strip of fusible web the same width as the finished belt carrier will be.

Place the fusible web slightly off center on the wrong side of the belt carrier strip.

Press the long edges of fabric over the web to fuse them so that the raw edge of the fabric is covered by the selvage.

Cut the strip into pieces the length of each carrier plus seam allowances.

APPLICATION OF BELT CARRIERS

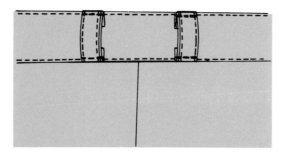

Topstitch by folding the carrier ends under.

Place them on your garment and stitch through all thicknesses.

- Or, if you prefer a belt carrier that does not have topstitching, use a hidden stitch technique, such as whipstitching.

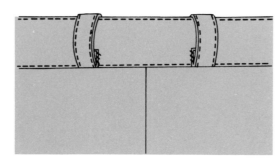

Whipstitch by folding the carrier ends under and stitching only the turned back ends to the garment. See Hand Sewing, page 81.

- On pants or skirt waistbands you can fold the top end over the waistband edge and whipstitch on the inside of the waistband.

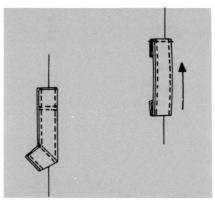

Machine stitch by placing one end of the carrier face down over the placement marking and stitching to the garment; then flip the carrier up.

Turn the end in and whipstitch or topstitch in place.

thread belt carriers

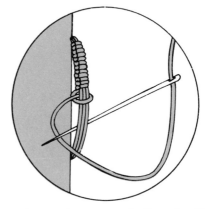

If you want a much narrower belt carrier, it's simple to make one from buttonhole twist or several strands of regular thread. First form a thread loop; continue to pull a loop inside a loop until you have a belt carrier the desired length, plus an added length for attaching. For exact directions, see Hand Sewing, page 81.

bias

Bias is beautiful. It is a strip of fabric cut in the diagonal direction which can be used to cover cording, bind an edge or add a design detail in another way.

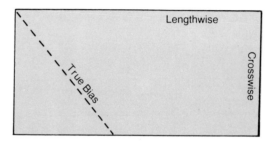

True Bias, which is on an exact 45° angle to the lengthwise and crosswise threads of the fabric, stretches easily. Because of this, you can use bias strips as trim on curved areas. The bias can be stretched slightly as you sew to help avoid puckers.

The method you choose to make bias trim depends on the amount you need. For large amounts, use the Continuous Bias Strip technique to prepare a fabric tube and then cut bias strips from it. For smaller lengths, locate the True Bias of your fabric, then cut bias strips and attach them end to end. This is called the Cut and Piece Method. Both techniques are equally simple and efficient.

continuous bias strip method

Cut a square or rectangle of fabric with the threads exactly on the lengthwise and crosswise grain on all four sides.

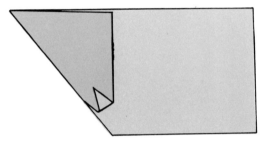

Fold one corner on the True Bias by matching the lengthwise grain with the crosswise grain.

Cut away the fabric end on the diagonal fold.

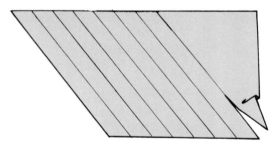

Mark slash lines the width of the bias trim required on the wrong side of the fabric.

- A width of 1½″ (38 mm) is best for most purposes.

Trim away the remaining diagonal end of fabric.

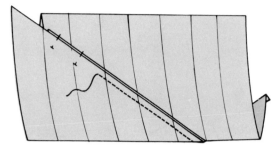

Pin baste the strip of fabric so the diagonal lines meet to form a tube.

- One width of bias should extend at each end of the tube.

- Note that the seam will spiral around the bias tube. This is fine, just pin baste carefully so you can sew the seam accurately.

Stitch a ¼″ (6 mm) seam allowance to sew the bias lengths together as a unit.

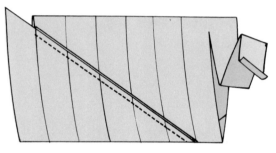

Cut bias strips as you need them.

cut and piece bias strip method

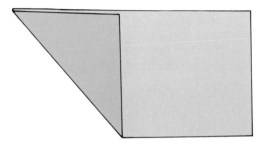

Fold a piece of fabric diagonally, placing the crosswise grain along the lengthwise grain.

- The folded diagonal line will be the True Bias.

Press along the fold to mark your first bias cutting line.

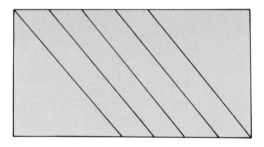

Mark the bias strips parallel to the folded crease using a ruler and a tracing wheel, tailor's chalk or a dressmaker's pencil.

- Bias strips 1½″ (38 mm) wide are ideal for most purposes.

Cut along the marked lines.

Pin baste the ends of the bias strips, right sides together.

To be certain that the strips are attached correctly to form a long bias piece, follow these simple steps.

1. Lay the strips next to each other, right sides up, with the matching cut ends side by side.

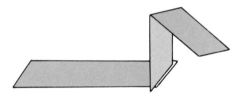

2. Flip one strip over and up so the strips are right sides together and at right angles, with small triangles extending.

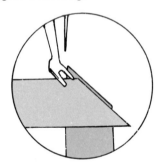

3. To sew the strips, the long ends of bias should extend to the left of the machine needle.

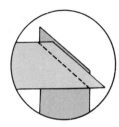

Stitch a ¼″ (6 mm) seam.

■ This attaches the strips so that the stitches are diagonal and suited to the stretchability of the bias.

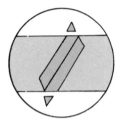

Press the seam open.

Trim the points.

welting

Welting is a bias strip folded flat and inserted into a seam. It is used as a fashion accent around pockets and necklines, along yoke seams or wherever you may want to add an interesting contrast.

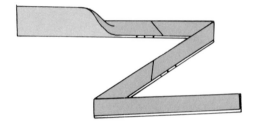

Cut a bias strip twice as wide as the finished welting *plus* 1¼″ (31 mm) to provide seam allowances.

Press the strip with wrong sides together to form a fold in the center which extends the entire length of the bias strip.

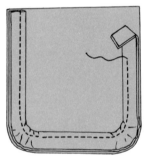

Place the bias strip in position to stitch it to the garment.

■ Be certain the cut edges of the garment and the welting strip are matched.

■ Use a seam guide on your machine to keep the stitching line even.

CORNERS AND CURVES

To turn a corner smoothly, you will need to clip the seam allowance of the bias strip to within 1/8″ (3 mm) of the seamline as you work. Follow these simple steps.

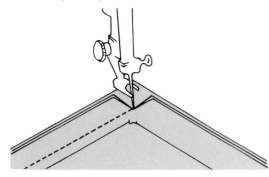

Stitch to the corner, leaving the sewing machine needle in the fabric.

Raise the presser foot.

Clip the seam allowance of the welting and pivot the fabric to begin stitching in a new direction.

Lower the presser foot and continue sewing.

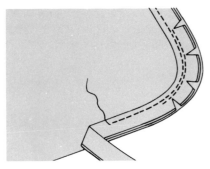

On curves, follow this same procedure to clip the seam allowance of the welting and the fabric. This will help the seam allowance lie flat. Reinforce curved areas with small machine stitches.

corded piping

Corded piping is a bias strip folded over cording. It is used as a fashion accent in the same way as welting.

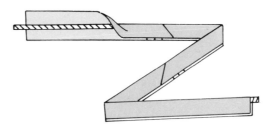

Cut the bias strip wide enough to wrap around the cording you've chosen *plus* 1¼″ (31 mm) to provide seam allowances.

Fold the bias strip around the cording so the lengthwise cut edges of the bias strip match.

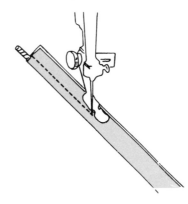

■ Use the zipper foot attachment on your sewing machine so you can stitch as close as possible to the base of the cording. This makes a snug, handsome trim.

■ Use large stitches, spaced closely enough to attach the bias strip but loose enough to be removed if necessary.

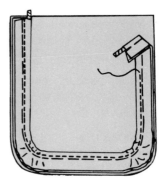

Stitch the corded piping to the right side of the garment so the stitching line which attached the bias strip around the cording rests exactly on the seam line and the cut edges match.

■ Use the zipper foot attachment on your sewing machine to sew just inside the original stitching line on the piping. This prevents these large stitches from showing on the finished garment.

■ Follow the same tips as for corners and curves, shown above.

corded tubing

Corded tubing is a bias strip that is stitched and turned with a cord inside. Since cording comes in all thicknesses, you can use it to make belts, button loops, shoulder straps and many other interesting fashion extras.

Cut a bias strip wide enough to wrap around the cord you have chosen *plus* 1¼" (31 mm) to provide seam allowances.

Cut the cord twice the length of your bias strip plus an additional inch (25 mm) to hold on to when you turn the tubing.

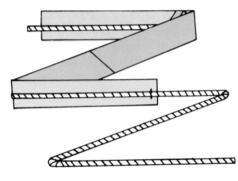

Place the cording on the wrong side of the bias strip, with the extra inch (25 mm) of cording extending over one end.

Stitch across the cord and bias at the center of the cord.

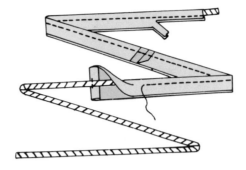

Fold the bias back over the cord, right sides together, matching the raw edges.

Stitch the bias close to the cord, using the zipper foot attachment of your machine, stretching the bias slightly as you sew.

- Use about 6-8 stitches per inch (each 25 mm) to sew the bias strip over the cording. This will prevent the stitches from popping when you shape the covered cording as it is sewn to an item.

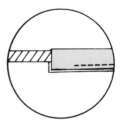

- Don't stitch into the small foldback at the end. It will be easier to turn if there is no stitching at that point.

Trim the seam allowances to within ⅛" (3 mm) of the stitching line.

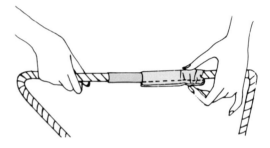

Turn the bias by pulling the fabric right side out over the cord.

- Pull gently, holding the end of the cord in one hand and working the fabric along with the other. The foldback will give you the start you need to turn the fabric easily.

bias tubing

Bias tubing is a bias strip stitched and turned right side out. Essentially, it is the same as corded tubing, without the cord. Use it to make the skinny tubing you need for button loops, spaghetti straps and other nice and narrow fashion trims. You can make bias tubing by following the directions for corded tubing. When you finish, just cut off the end to free the cord and pull it out, or follow these short, simple steps.

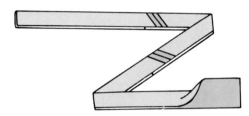

Cut a bias strip twice the desired finished width of the tubing *plus* 1¼" (31 mm) to provide seam allowances.

Fold the right sides together, matching the long raw edges.

Stitch down the length of the bias, using a seam gauge attached to your machine to keep the tubing the exact width you have planned.

■ Remember to stretch the bias slightly as you sew. Your stitches must be long enough to prevent them from popping when you turn the tubing.

Trim the seam allowances to ⅛" (3 mm) from the stitching line.

Turn the bias by slipping the bias tube into a loop turner.

■ A loop turner is a handy device which you can buy in any notions store. Use this special hook to catch one end of the trimmed tube and turn it right side out.

bindings

Bindings do double duty. They are narrow trims used to cover the raw edges of a garment and they also add a decorative touch. In short, they give a fashion finish.

You may already know something about bias bindings which you can make yourself using the Continuous Bias Strip Method or the Cut and Piece Bias Strip Method. Refer to page 31.

But bindings can also be bought. A wonderful assortment of colors, sizes and styles is available in stores which sell sewing notions. Single-fold and double-fold bias tape or single-fold braid trim are the main types of binding sold.

Any of these trims can be attached using one or more of the following simple techniques: Double Binding Method, Single Binding Method or Slip-On Binding Method. Learn how to do each one so you'll be able to add practical, professional-looking trims to your garments, accessories or decorator items.

double binding method

Cut a bias strip four times as wide as the width of the finished binding *plus* 1¼" (31 mm) to provide seam allowances.

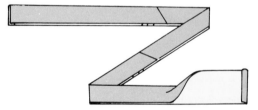

Fold the binding in half, wrong sides together.

- Turn under the ends of the binding to finish the raw edges when necessary.

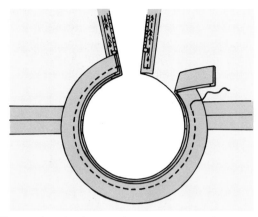

Place the binding on the wrong side of your garment, matching seamlines, and stitch it in position along the seamline.

Trim, grade, clip or notch the seam allowances as necessary.

- Refer to Seams, page 120.

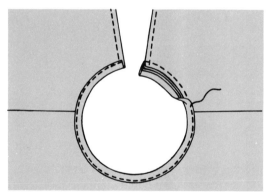

Flip the binding over the raw edges to the right side of the garment and edgestitch carefully, very near the fold, to attach the binding securely to the garment.

Edgestitch the binding to attach it to the garment.

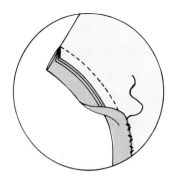

If you prefer, you can apply the binding without edgestitching. Stitch the bias to the right side of the garment, flip it to the wrong side and slipstitch it instead.

single binding method

Use purchased single-fold bias tape or bias strips you cut yourself. Your pattern envelope will describe the exact size of bias tape you need. Bias which you cut from fabric must be twice the width of the finished binding *plus* 1¼″ (31 mm) to provide seam allowances.

If you are using single-fold bias tape which you bought, gently press one long side open.

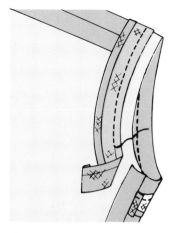

Place the right side of the binding on the wrong side of the garment.

- The crease line closest to the raw edge of the binding should be on top of the garment seamline.

- Turn under the ends of the binding to finish the raw edges when necessary.

Stitch in the crease line of the binding to attach it to the garment.

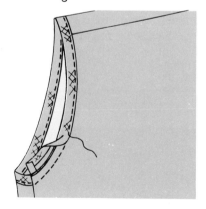

Flip the binding over the raw edges to the right side of the garment and edgestitch carefully, very near the fold, to attach the binding securely to the garment.

slip-on binding method

Use single-fold braid trim or double-fold bias tape for this fast and easy binding method.

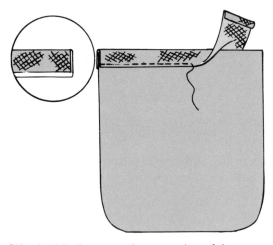

Slip the binding over the raw edge of the garment.

- Most double-fold bias tapes and fold-over braids have one edge slightly wider than the other. Always attach the binding so that the wider edge is on the wrong side of the garment. This allows you to catch both edges as you edgestitch from the right side.

- Open the fold of the binding and turn under the ends to finish the raw edges when necessary.

Edgestitch the binding from the right side of the garment.

corners and curves

The secret to sharp, crisp corners on your finished garment is in mitering.

For smooth, even curves, it is important to preshape the binding. Choose your binding method and follow these suggestions for perfect corners and curves.

DOUBLE AND SINGLE BINDING METHOD FOR OUTWARD CORNERS

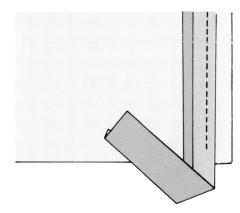

Stitch the binding to the point where the seamlines cross.

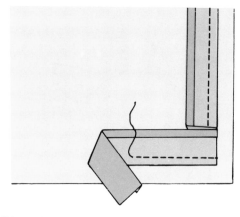

Place the binding along the opposite edge, forming a diagonal fold at the corner.

Stitch along the seamline.

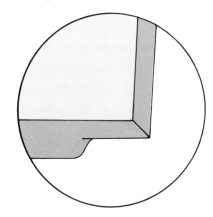

Fold the binding over the raw edges to the other side, forming a neat miter or diagonal fold on both sides of the garment.

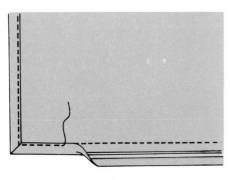

Finish the binding by slipstitching or edgestitching.

DOUBLE AND SINGLE BINDING METHOD FOR INWARD CORNERS

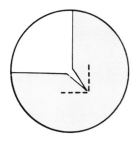

Reinforce the corner with small machine stitches, approximately 15-20 per inch (each 25 mm).

Clip into the corner, but not through the stitches.

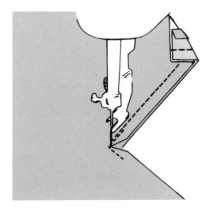

Stitch the binding to the garment up to the clip.

Lower the needle and raise the presser foot.

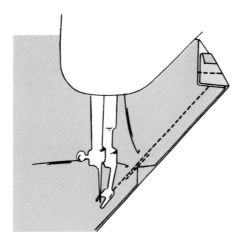

Spread the clipped corner to form a straight edge, matching the seamline of the binding and the garment.

Lower the presser foot and continue stitching.

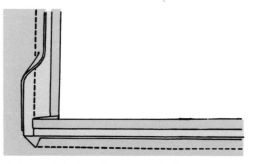

Fold the binding diagonally to form a miter at the corner.

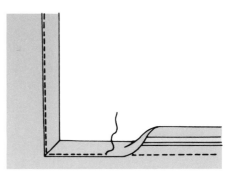

Turn the binding over the edge, forming a miter on the other side, and press.

Finish the binding by edgestitching or slipstitching.

SLIP-ON BINDING METHOD FOR OUTWARD CORNERS

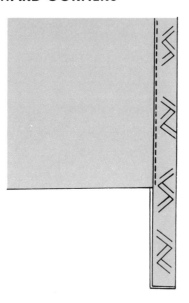

Stitch the binding to one garment edge.

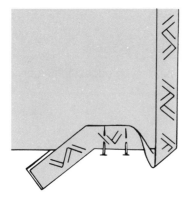

Bring the binding around the corner and pin it in place.

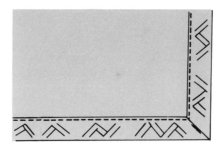

Form a neat miter at the corner and pin it in place

Stitch along the inside edge.

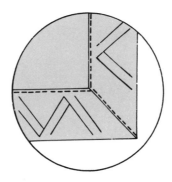

Edgestitch or slipstitch along the mitered fold to secure it.

SLIP-ON BINDING METHOD FOR INWARD CORNERS

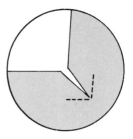

Reinforce the corner with small machine stitches, approximately 15-20 per inch (each 25 mm).

Clip into the corner, but not through the stitches.

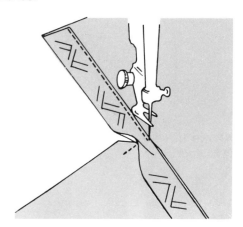

Slip the binding over one edge and stitch to the clip.

Raise the presser foot with the needle in the fabric.

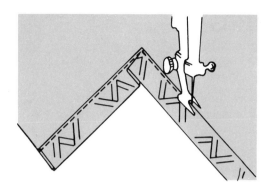

Slip the binding over the other edge, lower the presser foot and continue stitching.

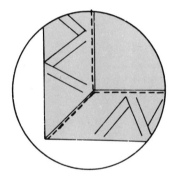

Form a neat miter at the corner.

Edgestitch along the mitered fold if necessary.

BINDING CURVES

Before applying binding to curves, shape it by pressing it to match the seamlines of the garment. The steam from your iron will help shrink out excess fullness to prevent tucks or puckers.

buttons and buttonholes

In the beginning, buttons were just for beauty.

From historic records it appears that buttons were invented about 1100 B.C. They were used mainly for decoration. Egyptians hung them on chains to make necklaces. Greeks and Romans used buttons for badges or clasps on their robes.

Finally, centuries later, in about 1200 A.D., an anonymous tailor invented buttonholes and buttons became useful as clothing fasteners.

BUTTONS

There are two basic types of buttons, sew-through and shank buttons.

- Sew-through buttons have holes or "eyes." To apply them, you sew right through the button itself as you attach it to the garment.

- Shank buttons don't have eyes. Instead they have a shank or ring on the back of the button so you can sew through the shank without your stitches showing on the face of the button.

PLACEMENT

Buttons should be placed according to the markings on your pattern. Their exact location depends on where the button will be used, the size of the button and design of the garment.

Before the buttons are attached, buttonholes must be made. For instructions, follow your pattern guidesheet or refer to the general steps described on page 44.

Once the buttonholes are completed, sew the buttons where they belong.

Place the side of the garment which has the buttonholes over the other side, in the same position it would be in if the garment was being worn.

- Be sure that the center lines of each side of the garment rest on top of one another.

Pin the garment sections together.

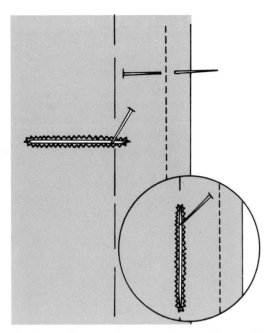

Mark your button placement by pushing a pin straight through the buttonhole ⅛″ (3 mm) from the outer end of a horizontal buttonhole or ⅛″ (3 mm) from the top of a vertical buttonhole.

sew-through buttons

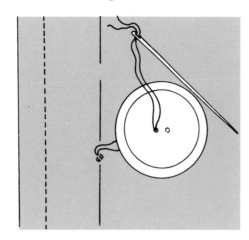

Backstitch tack on the right side of the garment directly on the mark for the button, using a double strand of thread.

- To strengthen the thread and prevent it from knotting while you're sewing, pull the thread through a piece of beeswax.

Place a pin or toothpick on top of the button to provide the necessary thread shank for the finished button.

- This thread shank allows some space between the garment and the button so that when the button is resting in the buttonhole, it will not be so tight that it causes puckers.

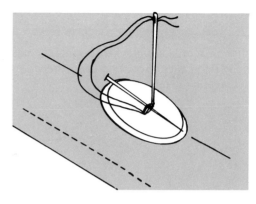

Stitch the button in place by sewing through the holes and over the pin or toothpick.

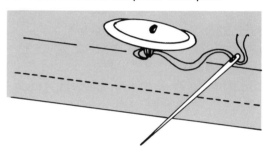

Remove the pin or toothpick and raise the button to the top of the stitches, winding the thread around the stitches under the button to strengthen the thread shank.

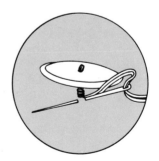

Backstitch into the fabric to secure the thread, then clip it close to the garment.

shank buttons

These buttons already have a metal or plastic loop on the back to provide space between the button and the fabric.

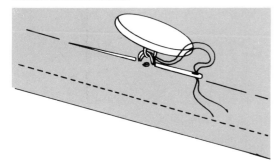

Backstitch tack on the right side of the garment, directly on the mark for the button, using a double strand of thread.

Stitch through the shank to attach the button with small, even stitches.

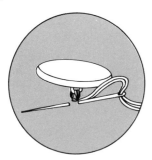

Backstitch into the fabric to secure the thread, then clip it close to the garment.

SEWING ON BUTTONS BY MACHINE

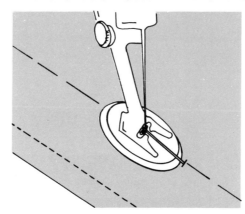

If you have several buttons to sew, you can do it quickly with your zigzag machine.

Turn your stitch length to "0," or set your machine so there is no movement of the fabric.

Place the button, with the pin or toothpick on top, under the pressure foot.

- Some machines have special attachments for this.

Set your zigzag width to hit the "eyes" of your button and stitch.

BUTTONHOLES

You can make many types of buttonholes using any of these methods: Machine Zigzag, Stitch and Slit, Hand-Worked and Bound Buttonhole. Imagine, you can learn a skill which even the most talented ancient scholars never dreamed about! You'll be surprised how simple making buttonholes can be.

LENGTH

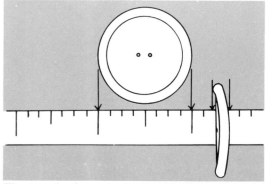

The length of your buttonhole is determined by the size of your button. The opening should be the diameter of the button, plus its thickness. Your pattern tissue has buttonhole markings equal to the diameter of the suggested button size plus 1/8" (3 mm).

PLACEMENT

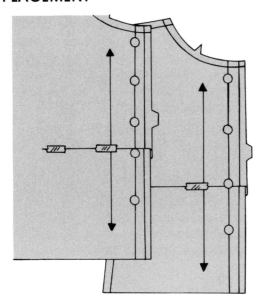

If you have made any pattern adjustments to lengthen or shorten the area where buttonholes are located, you may have to make new markings to indicate where the buttonholes belong. Keep the top and bottom buttonholes where they are and space the remaining ones evenly between them. If you have added a great deal to the original length, you may want to add an additional buttonhole to keep the buttons close enough to hold the garment securely and give it a balanced look.

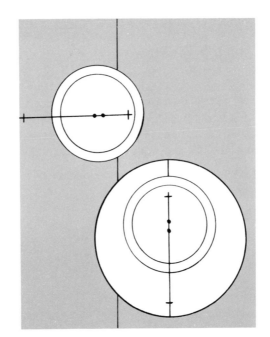

Horizontal buttonholes are placed ⅛″ (3 mm) out from the center line to allow room for the shank of the button. Vertical buttonholes are placed directly on the center line.

Use vertical buttonholes on knits whenever possible, because the lengthwise grain has less stretch than the crosswise grain and the stitching required to make the buttonholes will be less likely to cause puckers.

MARKING

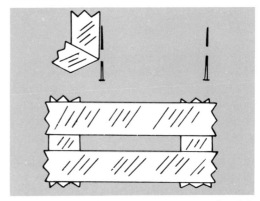

Buttonhole markings must appear on the right side of the fabric since the buttonholes will be made with the right side facing up. Because of this, it is important to choose a marking method which will not leave a permanent line on the fabric.

You can mark the buttonhole locations with pins, but this isn't always the best method. The pins do not stay exactly in place as you work and may get in your way as you try to stitch.

Hand basting is a quick and efficient method for marking the placement of buttonholes. Use a contrasting thread and nice, long stitches.

Also, you can buy a special tape which is used for sewing. It can be pressed lightly onto the fabric as a guide and then removed when the buttonholes are completed.

Then again, you can use tailor's chalk or a dressmaker's marking pencil. Always test a swatch of fabric first, to be sure that the marks you make can be removed easily. For more information about Marking, see page 13.

45

machine zigzag buttonholes

Buttonholes can be made easily on zigzag sewing machines. Many models have built-in buttonhole attachments; others are operated manually by changing the zigzag stitch width. Special buttonhole attachments can also be purchased for most machines.

Machine zigzag buttonholes are suitable for most garments or fabrics. They are made at the final stage of construction when all bands, facings or bindings have been completed.

Practice until you have mastered making buttonholes on your machine. Each machine is different, so follow your sewing machine manual carefully.

Mark the location of your buttonholes on the right side of the garment.

Follow the specific instructions in your sewing machine manual to sew the buttonhole accurately.

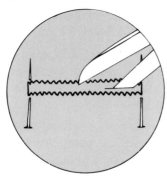

Cut through the center of the buttonhole, being careful not to cut into any zigzag stitches.

■ Place a pin at each end of the buttonhole to prevent cutting too far, and use only the points of your scissors.

stitch and slit buttonhole

The Stitch and Slit Buttonhole Method can be used successfully on any fabrics that don't fray —for example, felt, vinyl or natural or synthetic leathers or suedes. It eliminates unnecessary bulk, and is a fast, easy buttonhole to make.

Mark the fabric to indicate the location of each buttonhole.

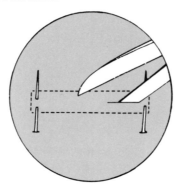

Stitch a narrow rectangle the exact size of your finished buttonhole through all the layers of fabric to reinforce the area.

Make a single slit through all the layers of fabric, inside the stitched rectangle.

■ Place a pin at each end of the buttonhole to prevent cutting too far, and use only the points of your scissors.

hand-worked buttonholes

When a zigzag machine is not available, or when you choose to make your buttonholes by hand, use the following method for perfect hand-worked buttonholes.

Mark the fabric to indicate the location of each buttonhole.

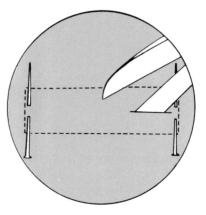

Stitch a rectangle the size of your finished buttonhole through all the thicknesses of fabric to reinforce the area and to serve as a guide for the depth of the hand stitches around your buttonhole.

Cut through the center of the reinforcement stitches through all thicknesses.

■ Place a pin at each end of the buttonhole to prevent cutting too far, and use only the points of your scissors.

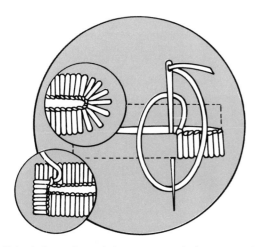

Stitch from the reinforcement stitches over the cut edge with a buttonhole stitch. Refer to Hand Sewing, page 78.

- Use buttonhole twist or a double strand of regular sewing thread.

- Your stitches should be evenly spaced and the same depth all around.

Finish the ends by making the stitches fan out around the ends or sewing a bartack at each end.

bound buttonholes

Bound buttonholes, most often used on tailored garments, are made by stitching a patch of fabric to the garment to form two lips. They are not suitable for sheer or delicate fabrics where the patch may show through.

Follow our instructions for the Five Line Method, it is the simplest way to make perfect bound buttonholes!

Apply the interfacing, but not the facing, before you make your bound buttonholes.

Cut patches of fabric about 2″ (50 mm) longer than the finished buttonhole and 2½″ wide (60 mm).

- Cut the patches on either straight grain or True Bias.

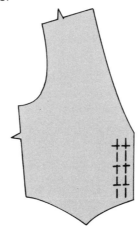

Mark the center line and the sides of the buttonholes on the right side of the fabric with thread markings, using either hand or machine basting.

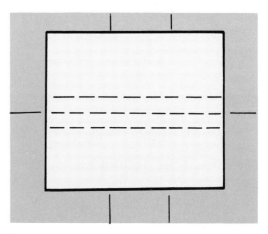

Place the patch and the garment right sides together, centering the patch over the buttonhole marking.

Baste three lines, first through the center marking and then ¼″ (6 mm) on each side of the center line.

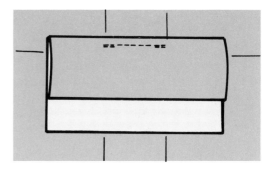

Fold the top of the patch downward toward the center to form a fold along the top basting line.

Stitch ⅛″ (3 mm) from this fold, using about 20 stitches per inch (each stitch approximately 1.5 mm) to secure the top of the buttonhole.

- Backstitch at the ends to reinforce these areas.

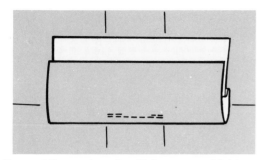

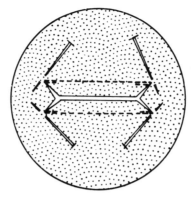

Repeat these steps to stitch a second fold as illustrated.

■ Check all the stitching lines for accuracy, length and spacing.

Remove the three basting lines.

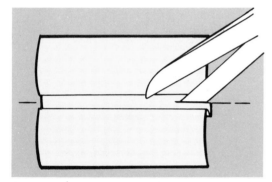

Cut the patch directly through the center.

■ Do not cut through the garment.

Turn the garment to the wrong side so that the stitches are in clear view.

■ Place a pin at each end of the buttonhole to prevent cutting too far, and use only the points of your scissors.

Cut the garment fabric and interfacing along the center of the buttonhole and into the corners to form a "V."

■ Cut all the way into the corners, but not through the stitches. Be careful not to cut into the patch.

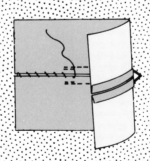

Pull the patch through to the wrong side and fold the small "V" at the ends away from the opening.

Whipstitch the buttonhole lips together.

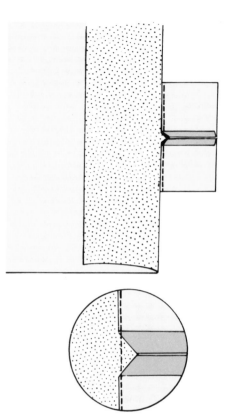

Fold the garment fabric back until you see the "V" at one end of the buttonhole.

Stitch through the patch to form the end of the buttonhole.

■ Stitching should cross the "V" at its widest point, extending about 1/8″ (3 mm) above and below it.

Repeat this step to complete the remaining end of the buttonhole.

Press the buttonhole from the wrong side of the garment so that all layers of fabric lie flat.

FINISHING THE FACING OF BOUND BUTTONHOLES

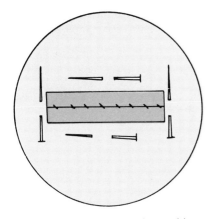

Pin baste the facing securely in position on the wrong side of the garment over the buttonhole area.

■ If your fabric is loosely woven, reinforce the facing area of each buttonhole with a piece of fusible interfacing.

Turn the slashed edge of the facing under and slipstitch it to the garment.

■ The turn will curve toward each end of the buttonhole forming an oval opening. Make a few extra small stitches to secure the ends.

Remove the whipstitching from the buttonhole lips and your buttonhole is complete.

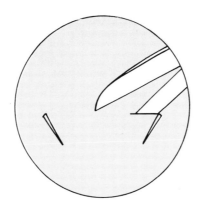

Slash the facing between the pins across the center of the buttonhole.

Turn the slashed edge of the facing under and slipstitch it to the garment.

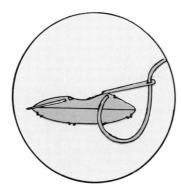

■ The turn will curve toward each end of the buttonhole forming an oval opening. Make a few extra small stitches to secure the ends.

Remove the whipstitching from the buttonhole lips and your buttonhole is complete.

casings

Casings are one of the most simple and useful items you can learn to sew.

A casing is a closed tunnel of fabric with a drawstring or piece of elastic inside to help control fullness. They're often used at sleeve edges, necklines or waistlines.

Both of the basic types of casing are easy to make.

- Applied Casings are made by sewing a separate strip of fabric to a garment.
- Folded Casings are formed by folding over an edge of the garment and stitching.

Be sure to count on casings when you think about creative details you can include on the garments you sew.

applied casings

Applied casings can be added to a project using a separate strip of fabric, either cut on the bias or on the straight grain. Single-fold bias tape which you can buy is also handy for an applied casing.

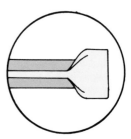

If you use a strip of fabric you've cut yourself, you have to fold the long edges to the wrong side along the seamline and press them in position before you begin. Single-fold bias tape already has the long edges folded in place.

Next, apply the casing using the Off The Edge or On The Edge Method, depending on where the casing is placed on your garment.

OFF THE EDGE

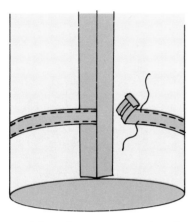

Pin the casing to the garment, using the placement markings on your pattern.

Turn under the ends of the casing so the folds meet without overlapping.

Edgestitch along both long edges.

ON THE EDGE

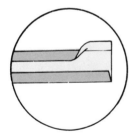

Press open one long edge of the casing.

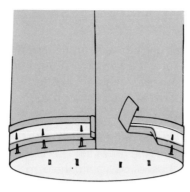

Pin the crease line of the casing along the seamline of the garment, right sides together.

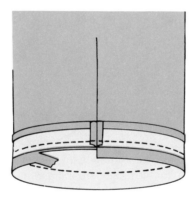

Stitch along the crease lines of the casing.

Trim the seam allowances.

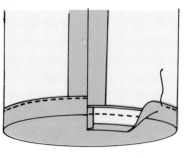

Flip the casing to the inside of the garment and press.

Edgestitch the other edge of the casing to the garment.

folded casings

Folded casings are similar to hems. They are extensions of the garment which are folded to the inside and stitched in position.

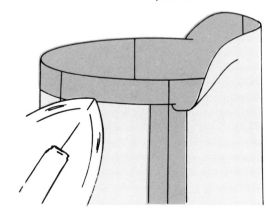

Turn the raw edge under ¼" (6 mm) and press.

Press your garment along the foldlines marked on your pattern tissue.

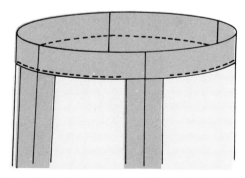

Edgestitch the fold nearest the cut edge to form the casing.

■ Leave a small space between the beginning and end of your stitches to insert a drawstring or elastic as necessary.

drawstrings

Drawstrings can be made from many different things. Refer to the section on Easy Fun Belts, page 28, for some ideas. Your pattern guidesheet will explain how long your drawstring must be.

Naturally, you will need an opening in the garment to pull the drawstring through. This opening either will be a buttonhole or a reinforced seam opening. Follow your pattern guidesheet and these simple hints.

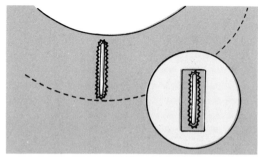

If your pattern recommends the use of a buttonhole for the casing opening, make the buttonhole before you attach the casing in its final position. It's a wise idea to reinforce the buttonhole area with a piece of fusible interfacing or seam tape. For additional buttonhole hints, see Buttonholes, page 44.

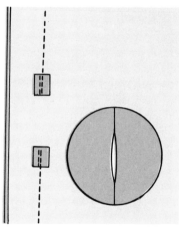

Casing openings which are in a seam are made as you stitch the seam. Your pattern guidesheet will have markings to show you the location. Reinforce the opening by placing small squares of seam binding or lightweight fabric along the edges on the inside of the garment and backstitching them.

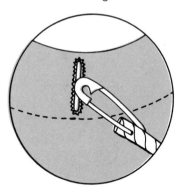

Then use a large safety pin to pull the drawstring through the casing.

elastic

Depending on the design of your garment, you may be using elastic in your casing. There are many types available, including "no-roll" elastic for waistlines and even a specially treated elastic for swimwear. Your pattern guidesheet will give specific directions for cutting a length of elastic just the right size for your needs.

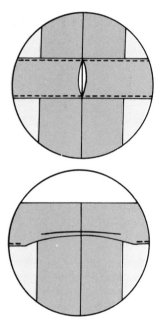

Leave an opening for inserting the elastic at the ends on an applied casing and along the stitched edge on a folded casing.

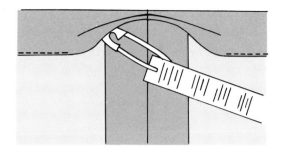

Insert the elastic with a safety pin, being careful not to twist it inside the casing.

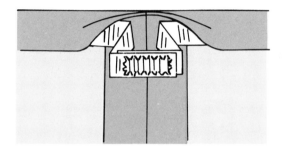

Overlap the ends of the elastic and stitch securely by machine after you have pulled it through the casing.

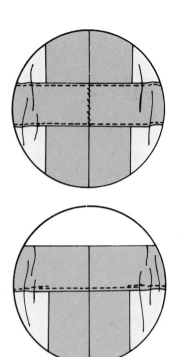

Finish the opening of an applied casing by slipstitching along the folded ends.

Finish the opening of a folded casing by completing the edgestitching.

Refer to Waistline Finishes, page 145, for more information about casings.

collars

Collars come as you like them, in many sizes and shapes, each designed to flatter a certain face or accent a particular fashion.

In this section you'll learn three easy ways to make good-looking collars: the Sandwiched Method, the Edgestitched Method and the Partially Sandwiched Method.

interfacing

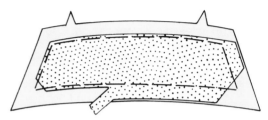

Interfacing will give your collar the added support it needs for a more professional look. For information on choosing and applying it, refer to Interfacing, page 86. Then follow these hints for professional results.

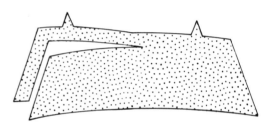

Eliminate bulk in the seams by using a fusible interfacing. Trim away the seam allowances from the interfacing piece before it is applied to the collar.

For knits, use a fusible interfacing on the upper collar. This prevents pulling and sagging of the fabric and results in a smoother-looking collar.

corners and curves

Corners and curves can make or break your collar. Pointed curves or rounded corners will make your collar less than perfect. Follow these guidelines to guarantee yourself success every time.

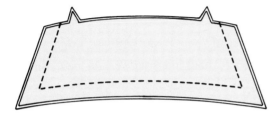

Begin stitching at the center back and stitch to the center front to prevent the points from curling in opposite directions.

- Refer to Machine Stitching, page 93, for more information on directional stitching.

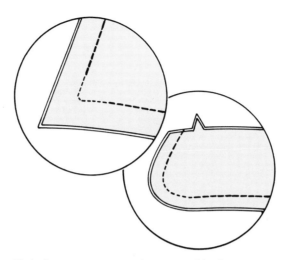

Reinforce corners and curves with shorter stitches, approximately 15-20 per inch (each 25 mm).

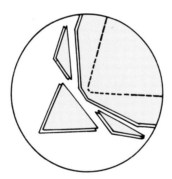

Take one small stitch across the point at corners.

- This allows you to trim the seam allowances closer so there is a bit more room and a bit less bulk when you turn the collar.

Trim the seam allowance close at the corners to prevent the fabric from bunching up.

- This method helps create the crisp, sharp collar points that are a sign of excellent sewing skills.

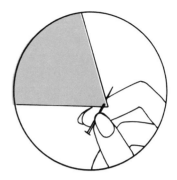

Use a needle or pin to pull the corners to a point.

- Never poke them out with your scissors or you may poke a hole right through the fabric.

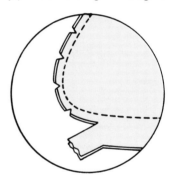

Trim and clip the seam allowances on curves for a smooth turn.

the undercollar

The undercollar plays an important part in the total success of the perfect collar. To prevent your undercollar from rolling out around the edges, follow these steps.

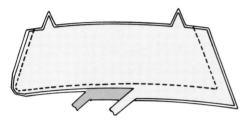

Grade and clip the seam allowances along the collar edges to eliminate bulk.

Understitch the undercollar to the seam allowances.

- For more information on understitching, refer to Machine Stitching, page 97.

Press the collar, rolling the seam slightly to the undercollar side.

- Now the undercollar will extend a bit beyond the uppercollar at the neckline edge.

Trim the undercollar edge so that it is a slight bit narrower than before, and matches the uppercollar edge exactly.

Stitch the uppercollar and undercollar together, using the recommended seam allowances from the pattern pieces.

SANDWICHED METHOD

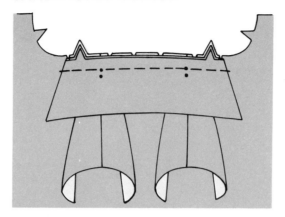

Baste the collar to the garment, matching the notches and markings.

- The undercollar is next to the right side of the garment.

- The collar neckline has a different curve than that of the facing and garment.

Staystitch and clip the garment neckline seam allowances, if necessary, to make the neckline lie smoothly.

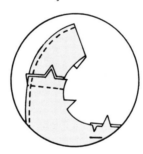

Join the back neck facing to the front facings.

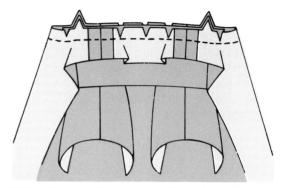

Stitch the neckline, sandwiching the collar between the garment and the facing.

Grade and clip the seam allowances.

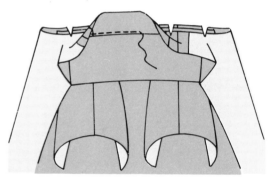

Understitch the facing to the seam allowance to prevent the facing from rolling out.

EDGESTITCHED METHOD

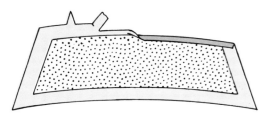

Make an edgestitched collar following your pattern guidesheet and these suggestions for perfect results.

Trim the seam allowance along the neckline of one collar section to ¼" (6 mm) from the seamline.

Press the trimmed edge to the wrong side of the collar along the seamline.

Stitch uppercollar to undercollar.

Turn right side out and press.

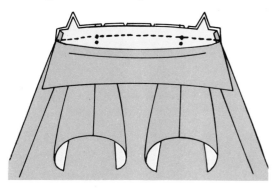

Stitch the untrimmed collar seam to the garment, matching all dots and notches carefully before you sew.

■ You can't make a mistake with this collar since you can stitch the collar to either the right or wrong side of the garment!

■ The collar neckline has a different curve than that of the facing and garment.

Staystitch and clip the collar neckline seam allowances, if necessary, to make the neckline lie smoothly.

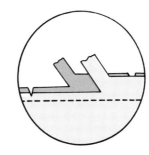

Grade and clip the seam allowances.

Place the unstitched edge of the collar over the seam allowances.

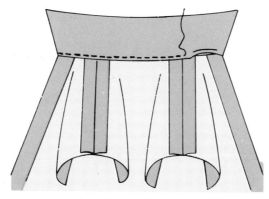

Edgestitch along the neckline seam through all thicknesses.

PARTIALLY SANDWICHED METHOD

As always, your best bet is to follow the directions on the pattern guidesheet for your garment. It will give you the details about these general steps for making a collar using the Partially Sandwiched Method.

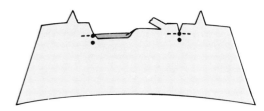

Clip the seam allowances of the upper collar section at the shoulder markings.

Trim the seam allowances between clips to ¼" (6 mm) from the seamline.

Press the trimmed edge to the wrong side along the seamline.

Stitch the uppercollar to the undercollar, turn right side out and press.

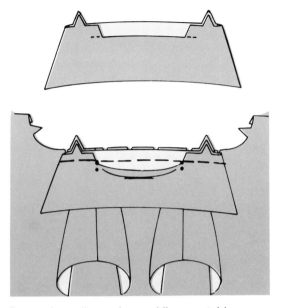

Baste the collar to the neckline, matching markings.

▪ Keep the trimmed edge free.

▪ The collar neckline has a different curve than that of the facing and garment.

Staystitch and clip the garment neckline seam allowances, if necessary, to make the neckline lie smoothly.

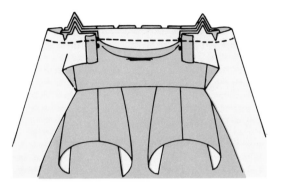

Fold the front facings over the collar and garment.

Stitch along seamline through all thicknesses, keeping the trimmed edge of the collar free as you sew.

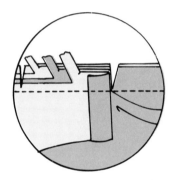

Grade the seam allowances and trim excess fabric from corners.

Clip the garment and collar seam allowances exactly at the end of the facing so that the collar will turn smoothly over the seam.

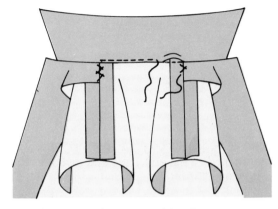

Turn facings to the wrong side of garment and press.

Place the unstitched part of the collar over the seam allowances.

Edgestitch along the neckline seam through all thicknesses.

Cross stitch the facing edges to the shoulder seams to keep the facing in position as the garment is worn.

cuffs

Cuffs add interest to any style of sleeve. Sometimes they are made of the same fabric used for the garment, other times they are created from contrasting colors, prints or plaids.

There are two basic categories of cuffs: Extended Cuffs and Fold-Up Cuffs.

■ An Extended Cuff is made from a separate piece of fabric attached to the bottom edge of a sleeve. Generally these cuffs help control fullness by holding the gathers of the sleeve pleat in position.

■ A Fold-Up-Cuff is formed just like a deep hem. The fabric is folded and held in position with small hand stitches or machine stitching.

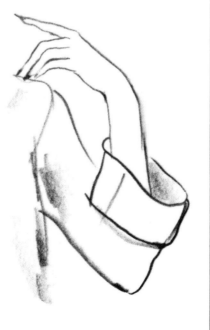

extended cuffs

Extended cuffs are further divided into two types: Buttoned Cuffs and Barrel Cuffs.

■ Buttoned Cuffs have opening plackets and are closed with buttons or some other fastener.

■ Barrel Cuffs have no opening and must be large enough to allow your hand to slip through easily.

BUTTONED CUFFS

Interface the cuff following your guidesheet and the instructions in Interfacing, page 86.

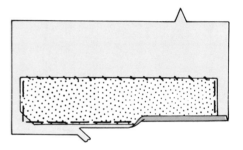

Trim the unnotched seam allowances of the cuff to ¼" (6 mm) from the seamline.

Press the trimmed edge to the wrong side along the seamline and baste if necessary.

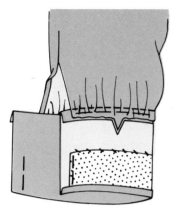

Stitch the right side of the cuff to the wrong side of the sleeve, matching markings.

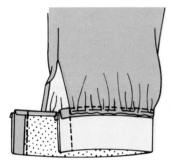

Fold the cuff, right sides together, and stitch the side seams of the cuff.

Grade the seam allowances of the side seams and trim the corners diagonally.

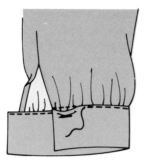

Turn the cuff, right sides out, matching the seamline of the trimmed edge to the first seam.

Edgestitch the cuff from the right side.

■ If you want the cuff finished so that the edgestitching doesn't show, stitch one side of the cuff to the right side of the sleeve, with the right sides of the fabric together.

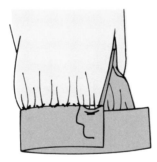

Then fold the cuff to the wrong side of the garment, press the seam allowances of the cuff in position and slipstitch along the seamline from the inside.

BARREL CUFFS

Interface the cuff following your guidesheet and the information in Interfacings, page 86.

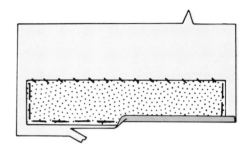

Trim the unnotched seam allowances of the cuff to ¼″ (6 mm) from the seamline.

Press the trimmed edge to the wrong side along the seamline and baste if necessary.

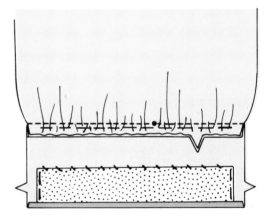

Stitch the cuff to the sleeve, right sides together.

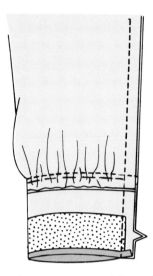

Stitch the underarm seam and the cuff seam, right sides together.

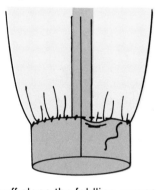

Fold the cuff along the foldline, wrong sides together.

Slipstitch from the inside.

fold-up cuffs

Fold-up cuffs are a design detail used at the bottom edge of pants and sleeves. They are made with a deep hem that is folded to the right side of the garment.

Just follow these basic steps to make great-looking fold-up cuffs, in a flash.

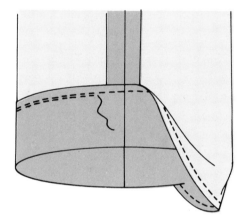

Finish the lower edge of the cuff.

■ Refer to Seam Finishes, page 121.

Fold the cuff along the foldline to the inside and hem.

■ The hem won't show, so it can be made quickly by machine stitching through all thicknesses.

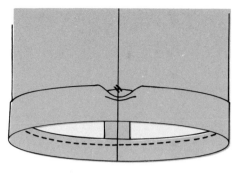

Fold the lower edge of the garment to the right side along the hemline.

Tack the cuff in place with a whipstitch at each seam.

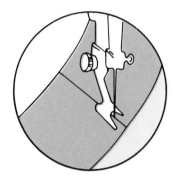

■ You can get the job done quickly if you "stitch-in-the-ditch." Simply stitch through all thicknesses in the ridge of the seam.

darts

Darts are wedge-shaped tucks which are sewn into fabric to help control and direct fullness. Darts allow fabric, which is flat, to be softly fashioned into garments that look attractive and feel comfortable.

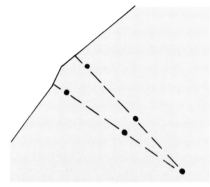

Work on the wrong side of your fabric.

Transfer the markings from the pattern tissue to your fabric using tracing paper, tailor's wax, tailor's chalk or another marking device which will not damage your fabric or leave a mark to show through on the right side of the finished garment. Refer to Marking, page 13, for more information.

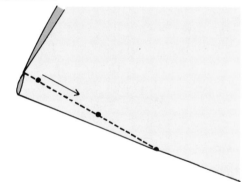

Fold the fabric, right sides together, and match the markings.

■ For extra accuracy, press along the fold before stitching.

Stitch from the wide end of the dart to the point.

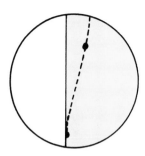

■ To prevent bubbles at the point of your darts, gradually curve your stitching line so that the final stitches fall along the folded edge.

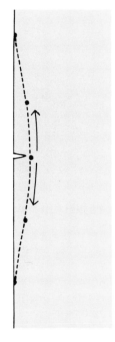

■ Some darts have two pointed ends. On these contour darts, start at the center and stitch to each point. This is an easy technique for making the points of the dart accurately. Sometimes contour darts require clipping to prevent puckering.

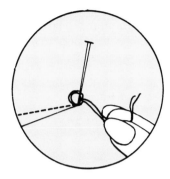

Tie the thread ends at the point to prevent the stitching from pulling out.

■ Place a pin at the point of the dart to control the knot. It will slide down the pin and tighten at the point of the dart.

Press the dart flat as stitched, then press it over a tailor's ham or pressing mitt to shape the garment.

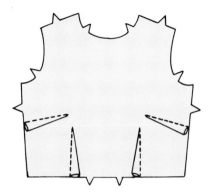

■ Always press a dart before you sew over it with another seam.

■ Darts which lie in a vertical position should be pressed so they face the center of the garment.

■ Darts which lie in a horizontal position should be pressed to face downward.

facings

A facing is a fabric section used to finish the cut edges of a garment. Facings are used most often at necklines, front or back openings, armholes and waistbands.

There are two types of facings: Shaped Facings and Bias Facings.

- Shaped Facings are cut in the exact shape of the area they finish.

- Bias Facings are made with bias strips stitched to the garment edge which then take on the shape of the garment opening.

shaped facings

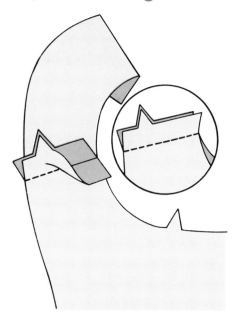

Join the facing sections by sewing them together along the seamlines shown on the pattern.

- Be certain that you match the notches accurately.

- In curved areas, the sections of a shaped facing will meet at the seamlines but not at the cut edge. However, when the facing is stitched to the garment, the edges will be evenly matched.

Finish the outside edge of the facing.

- Refer to Seam Finishes, page 121.

Stitch the facing to the garment, right sides together.

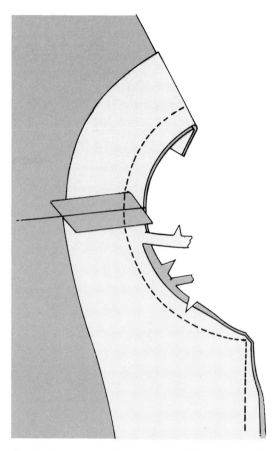

Grade the seam allowances and clip around curved areas.

■ Trim close to the stitching at corners.

Press the seam allowances open, then press them toward the facing.

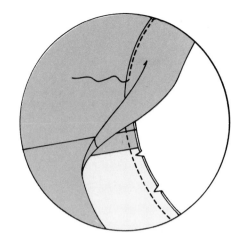

Understitch the seam allowances to the facings.

■ For information on understitching, refer to Machine Stitching, page 97.

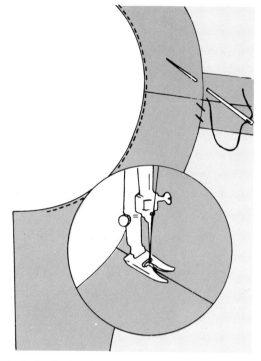

Tack the facing in place at the seams with a whipstitch or "stitch-in-the-ditch."

bias facings

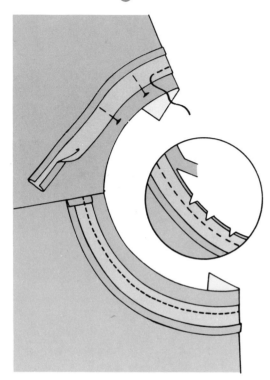

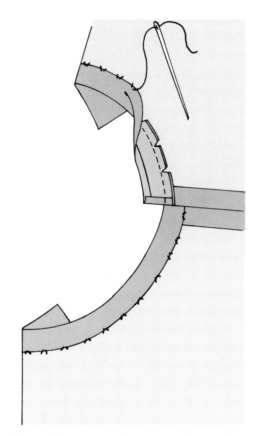

Open one long edge of the purchased bias tape.

Pin the crease line of the bias tape so that it rests on the seamline of the garment, right sides together.

■ Do not stretch the tape.

Stitch along the crease line of the bias tape to attach it to the garment, stretching the bias slightly as you sew to give a smooth appearance to the finished facing.

Trim and clip the seam allowance.

Flip the bias tape to the wrong side and press.

■ Make sure that none of the bias tape is showing from the right side.

Slipstitch the tape to the garment.

other facing methods

Some facings are designed to look like bands. Your pattern will give you exact instructions for making this special type of facing. Generally, the right side of the facing is stitched to the wrong side of the garment so the facing is inside the cut edge. For more facts about this type of facing, refer to Shaped Facings, page 64.

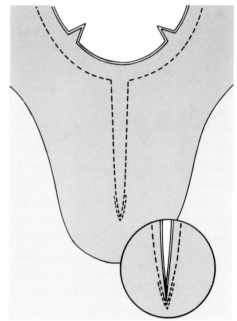

Remember to use extra care to reinforce facings which require a slash opening. Stitches should be small enough to provide a firm seam. Make a single stitch across the point of the slash as explained in Machine Stitching, page 98. Trim the seam allowances of the slash as close as possible, about 1/8″ (3 mm) from the stitching line. If necessary, clip to, but not through, the stitches so that the slash opening will lie flat when the garment is completed.

fasteners

Fasteners are devices such as hooks and eyes, snaps, ties or special nylon tapes which can be used alone or in combination with buttons to help close garments securely.

There is an endless variety of fasteners for many different purposes, some decorative as well as serviceable.

Always read your pattern envelope carefully to learn which type of fasteners are suggested for your garment.

Use this information as your guide or be a bit creative and choose another type of fastener. All fasteners are equally easy to apply and most of them work well in many situations.

Hooks and eyes are used most often at waistlines and necklines. They are available in a variety of sizes, including special heavy hooks for waistlines, where there is extra strain on the garment.

OVERLAPPING EDGES

Use a hook and a straight eye or a hook and a thread chain eye.

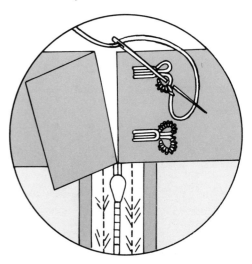

Place the hook on the inside of the overlap, about ¼″ (6 mm) from the edge.

Stitch around each hole with a buttonhole stitch.

■ See Hand Sewing, page 78.

Pass the needle through the middle of the hook.

Whipstitch the end of the hook to hold it flat against the fabric.

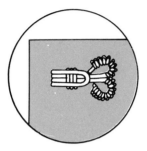

Backstitch tack to secure the end of the thread to the fabric and clip thread close to the garment.

■ To learn how to backstitch tack, see Hand Sewing, page 77.

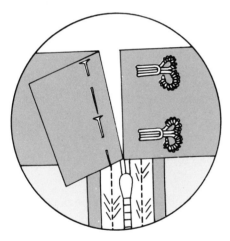

Mark the position of the eye on the other side of the garment by overlapping the garment edges and placing a pin where the end of the hook falls.

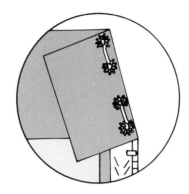

Stitch the straight eye in place with a buttonhole stitch around each hole.

■ See instructions, Hand Sewing, page 78.

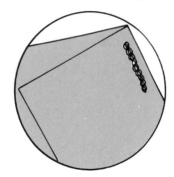

■ You can also make an eye with a thread chain by following the directions in Hand Sewing, page 81.

EDGES THAT MEET

Use a hook and a round eye or a hook and a thread chain eye.

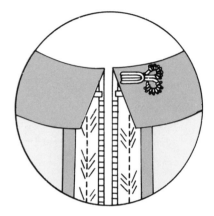

Place the hook on the inside of your garment, just a slight distance from the edge.

Stitch around each hole using a buttonhole stitch.

■ See instructions, Hand Sewing, page 78.

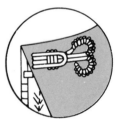

Pass the needle through the fabric to the middle of the hook.

Whipstitch the end of the hook to hold it flat against the fabric.

Backstitch tack to secure the end of the thread and clip it close to the garment.

- To learn how to backstitch tack, see Hand Sewing, page 77.

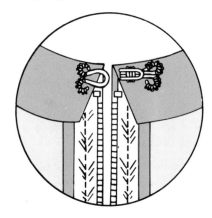

Place a round eye on the inside of the other edge so that the loop extends slightly beyond the edge.

- When the hook and eye are attached the garment edges should meet exactly.

Stitch the round eye in place with a buttonhole stitch around each hole.

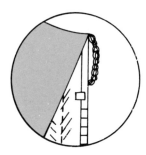

- You can also make an eye with a thread chain by following the directions in Hand Sewing, page 81.

snaps

Snaps are fasteners used to hold overlapping edges together. They are used at areas where there is a minimum amount of strain. A snap is made of two sections, the ball half and the socket half.

Snaps are available in a variety of sizes, including the heavy gripper snaps used for sportswear and children's clothes. Follow the manufacturer's instructions for applying gripper snaps and these directions for sewing the other type of snap onto a garment.

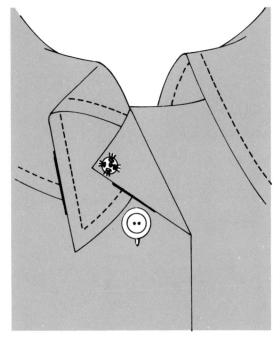

Place the ball half of the snap on the underside of the overlap, far enough from the edge so it will not show.

Buttonhole stitch through each hole, carrying the thread under the snap from hole to hole.

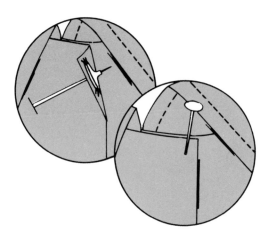

Mark the position of the socket half of the snap by overlapping the edges and pushing a pin through the ball of the snap.

- Or, rub tailor's chalk on the ball and press it against the opposite garment edge.

Buttonhole stitch the socket half of the snap in place, just as you did the ball half.

ties

Pull your best fashion ideas together with ties. Buy narrow cording to use as ties or make your own, following these directions.

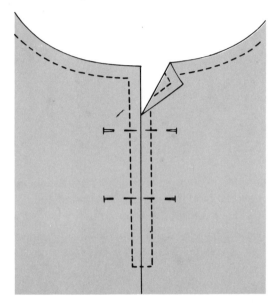

Match or overlap the garment edges which will be joined when the ties are in use.

Mark the placement for your ties.

Cut the ties to the desired length plus a seam allowance.

■ You can make your ties without fuss by following the Fold and Stitch Method in Belts, page 26.

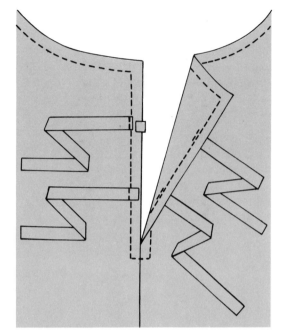

Stitch the tie to the marking and trim away the extra fabric.

■ This reduces bulk and gives you a nice and narrow tie, the exact length you want.

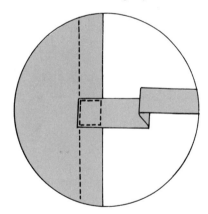

Flip the tie over the stitching and topstitch securely to the garment.

nylon tape fasteners

Nylon tape fasteners are a recent invention which allow you to make a fastener of just about any size or shape, as long or as short as you like.

The fastener itself is formed by two pieces of sturdy nylon fabric; one piece is loopy, the other is fuzzy. Place the loopy and the fuzzy pieces together and they hold on to one another to form a secure closing. Then, when you want to open the garment, simply peel the layers away from each other.

You may open and close the nylon tape fastener time and time again. It is very durable and can be washed or dry cleaned often.

Nylon tape fasteners are used on children's clothes, sportswear and many home furnishings or craft items. They work just about anywhere but are not recommended for very heavy or bulky fabrics.

Since nylon tape fasteners are sold in various sizes and also by the yard or meter, they are very useful.

APPLYING NYLON TAPE FASTENERS

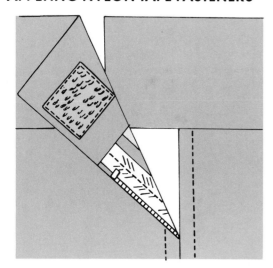

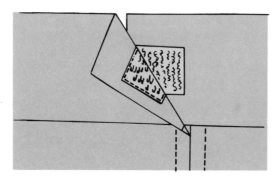

Mark and position the fuzzy half of the fastener on the other side of the opening.

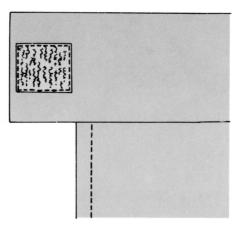

Place the loopy half of the fastener in position on the overlapping edge.

■ To be certain that the fastener is where it should be, close the garment as it will be when worn, mark the placement for the loopy nylon tape and then pin it to the fabric.

Stitch this half of the fastener to the garment, stitching through all fabric thicknesses.

Stitch this half of the fastener to the garment through all thicknesses.

gathering

Gathering helps control fabric fullness. You can gather using the Machine Gathering Method or the Instant Gathering Method, which is suitable for heavy fabrics or very long pieces such as bedspread sections.

Follow these steps to gather quickly and evenly.

machine gathering

Use long machine stitches, then pull them to gather up light or medium weight fabric for ruffles and other trims.

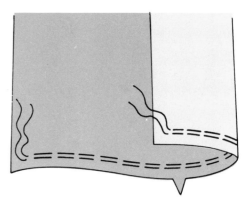

Machine baste two rows of stitches from the right side of your fabric—the first row on the seamline and the second ¼″ (6 mm) into the seam allowance.

■ Use long basting stitches, about 6-8 per inch (every 25 mm). The heavier the fabric, the longer the stitches should be.

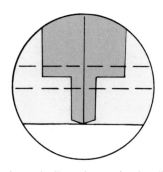

■ To eliminate bulk at the gathering line, trim any crossing seam allowances before basting.

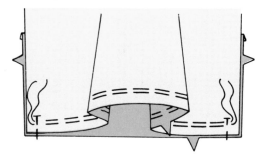

Match the markings and pin the fabric edges, right sides together.

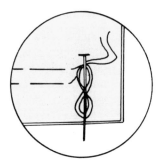

Secure the bobbin threads at one end of the fabric by winding them in a figure eight around a pin.

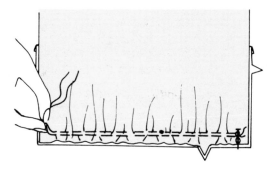

Pull the bobbin threads from the opposite end and gently slide the fabric along the thread to create soft, even gathers.

■ Adjust the gathers to create smooth, even folds.

Pin baste the gathered edge to the ungathered edge, matching notches.

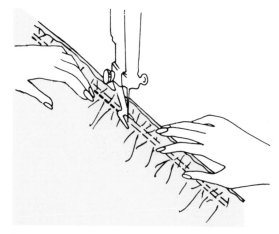

Stitch along the seamline, gathered side up.

■ Hold the gathers evenly on both sides of the needle to prevent catching any tucks in your seam.

instant gathering

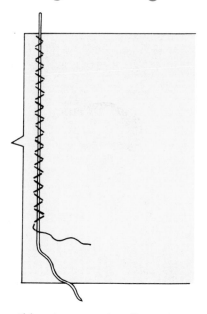

Place a thin, strong cord on the seam allowance, ¼" (6 mm) from the seamline.

Machine stitch with a wide zigzag stitch over the cord.

■ Be careful not to stitch into the cord. The zigzag stitch will form a loose casing which will hold the cord so it can be drawn up to gather the fabric.

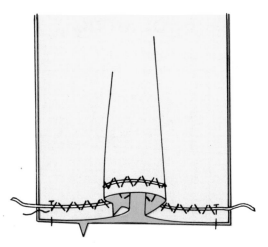

Match the markings and pin the fabric edges, right sides together.

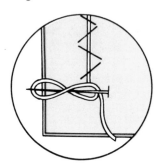

Secure one end of the cord by wrapping it in a figure eight around a pin.

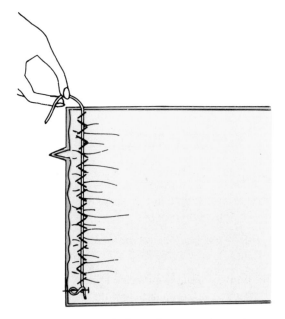

Pull the cord gently from the opposite end to form the gathers.

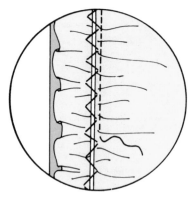

Stitch along the seamline, gathered side up.

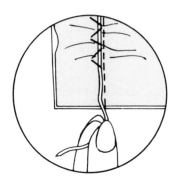

Remove the cord by removing the pin and pulling one end gently.

Some sewing machines have a special gathering or ruffler attachment. Refer to your sewing machine manual for instructions. Practice the recommended method on scraps of fabric until you have it mastered. Then, use gathered strips or ruffles as a pretty addition to many projects. Refer to Ruffles, page 110, for some ideas about putting these trims in their place on a garment or home furnishing item.

hand sewing

Even though modern sewing machines can do just about anything, you need to know the basics about sewing by hand with a needle and thread.

That's because almost every item you sew will require some hand stitches, either to finish a hem, attach fasteners or add a decorative trim.

Many experts enjoy sewing by hand. They believe it gives them an extra sense of creativity and adds a custom touch to their garments. You will too, once you learn the best hand-sewing techniques.

needles

Select a needle that is comfortable for you and the stitch you're using. Fine needles work best for most hand stitches; the longer the stitch, the longer the needle should be. Needles which are labeled "sharps," "betweens" or "crewel" are all good choices for hand sewing.

thread

There are many types of thread but all-purpose cotton, polyester or polyester/cotton, sizes 40 or 60, are the most useful threads for fine hand sewing.

Follow these hints for successful hand sewing.

1. Use a single strand of thread in most cases.

2. Use white or light-colored thread for basting, since a dark-colored thread may leave a dye stain on your fabric.

3. Cut thread on an angle. It will slide through the eye of your needle easier. Biting or breaking thread frays the ends and makes it difficult to thread your needle.

4. To avoid tangles or knots, cut your thread no longer than 18″-23″ (45-60 cm) and also pull it through beeswax. This is available in notions departments.

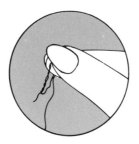

Hold the loop with your middle finger and your thumb.

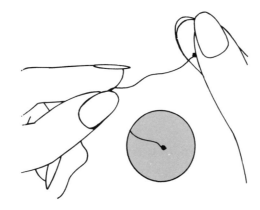

Pull on the thread to make the knot.

HAND-SEWING STITCHES

backstitch

This is one of the strongest hand stitches and often is used to repair seams. It's also a great stitch for applying patch pockets.

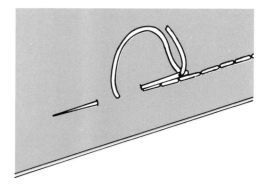

Secure the thread to the fabric on the seamline using a backstitch tack.

Insert the needle one short stitch length behind the thread.

Bring the needle out again, one stitch length ahead of the thread, on the seamline.

Continue stitching, one stitch behind and one ahead of the thread.

Finish by securing the thread with a backstitch tack.

5. If your thread twists as you sew, let it hang with the needle end down. Then run your thumb and index finger down along the thread to untwist it.

6. Thread is secured to a garment with a backstitch tack or a knot. Knot the end of your thread by following these steps.

Wrap the end of the thread around your index finger, holding it in place with your thumb.

Hold the thread taut and slide your index fingertip down your thumb.

■ The thread will twist slightly and the loop thus formed will slide off your finger.

backstitch tack

This stitch is used to attach the thread to the fabric at the beginning and the end of your hand stitches. It is stronger than knotting the thread and is preferred by most experts because it gives a durable, professional start or finish to a hand-sewn area.

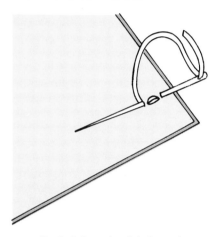

Take a small stitch into the fabric at the beginning point of your hand sewing.

Stitch several times over the first stitch to secure the thread.

bar tack

Bar tacks are usually positioned to reinforce an area where there is a good deal of strain on the seam, such as at the corners of pockets, the ends of hand-worked buttonholes and the bottom of fly front zippers.

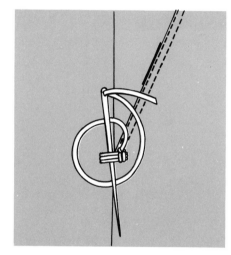

Make several overlapping stitches the desired length of the bar tack.

■ You can strengthen the bar tack by working closely spaced buttonhole stitches over it, catching the fabric underneath.

Finish by pulling the thread to the underside and securing it with a backstitch tack.

basting

This temporary stitching is used to hold layers of fabric together. Basting should be removed from the garment as soon as the seams are in place and it is no longer needed.

Knot the thread.

■ In this instance you can knot the thread without worrying about hiding the knot since the stitches will be removed.

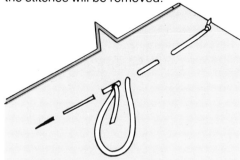

Take long uneven stitches, about 1″ (25 mm) apart and ¼″ (6 mm) long.

■ Save time by taking several stitches with your needle before pulling the thread through the fabric.

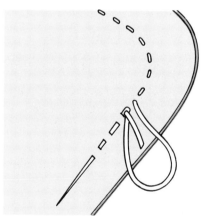

■ For areas where you need more control, such as curved seams, take short ¼″ (6 mm) stitches about ¼″ (6 mm) apart.

Continue the stitches to complete the seamline.

Finish by securing the thread with a very loose backstitch tack.

blindstitch

The name says it all. This is a stitch which is just about invisible from the right side of the garment. When the blindstitch is well done, no lumps, bumps or bubbles will ruin the look of the hem or facing.

Backstitch tack to attach the thread to the fabric.

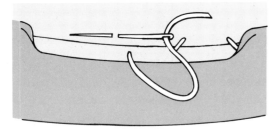

Take a small horizontal stitch through the garment to catch only one or two threads of the fabric.

Stitch diagonally to the hem or facing.

Continue, forming a very narrow zigzag stitch which is barely visible.

Finish by securing your thread with a backstitch tack.

buttonhole stitch

This stitch is used primarily to make hand-worked buttonholes but can also be used as a decorative finish on the edge of your fabric. Use buttonhole twist or a double strand of regular thread. Pull it through beeswax to help prevent twisting.

Secure the thread with a backstitch tack and bring your needle to the topside of the fabric.

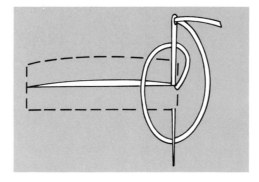

Loop the thread around the area of the stitch.

Stitch over the fabric edge from the underside to the topside into the loop.

■ Keep the loop under the needle at both ends.

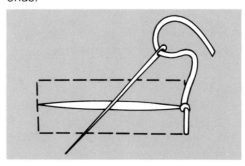

Pull the needle out of the fabric through the loop, forming a knot on the edge of the fabric.

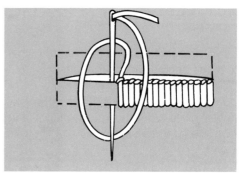

Stitch along the edge at the depth and spacing desired.

Finish by taking the thread to the underside of the fabric and securing it with a backstitch tack.

catchstitch

This diagonal stitch is used to hold two layers of fabric together in areas such as hems and facings.

Backstitch tack to attach the thread to the fabric.

Stitch from left to right with your needle pointing to the left.

■ If you are left-handed, you may want to stitch from right to left.

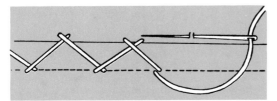

Make a small horizontal stitch in one layer of fabric, a short distance from the edge.

■ To prevent stitches from showing on the outside of the garment, be careful to pick up only one or two threads of fabric as you sew.

Make another horizontal stitch, just barely over the edge, on the other layer of your fabric.

Continue the stitches, forming a zigzag pattern, keeping the thread loose and relaxed.

Finish by securing the thread with a backstitch tack.

cross stitch

The cross stitch is used most often at the center back of a jacket or coat lining. Use a heavier thread such as buttonhole twist or a double strand of regular thread. The cross stitch may also be used as a decorative stitch.

Backstitch tack to attach the thread to the fabric.

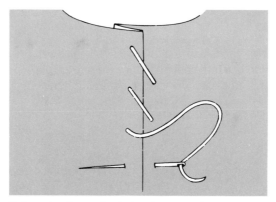

Take a horizontal stitch, about ¼"-⅜" (6-10 mm) wide.

Continue downward, making a row of horizontal stitches, spaced as far apart as they are long, forming a diagonal design.

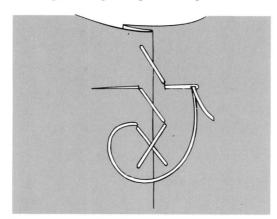

Reverse your direction by moving the thread up and over the diagonal stitches you have just made.

Continue making these horizontal stitches at the same location as the previous stitches to form an "X" design.

Finish by securing the thread with a backstitch tack.

cross stitch tack

The cross stitch tack, another version of the cross stitch, is used to hold an edge in place. You may find it useful at facing edges.

Backstitch tack to attach the thread to the fabric.

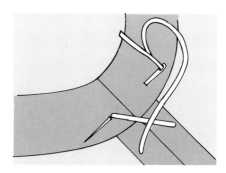

Make a cross stitch over the edge to be tacked.

■ Be sure that the stitches used for the cross stitch tack do not show on the outside of the garment.

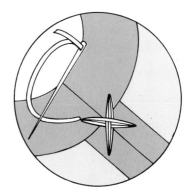

Continue making several cross stitches over the first one.

Finish by securing the thread with a backstitch tack.

slipstitch

An almost invisible stitch, the slipstitch is used to join two folded edges or one folded edge to a flat surface. It's great for skinny rolled hems and for attaching linings.

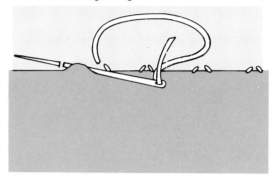

Secure the thread and bring the needle through the folded edge.

Slip the needle through the folded edge and, with the same stitch, catch one or two threads in the other layer of fabric.

Continue the stitches, always slipping the needle through the fold on the other layer of fabric.

Finish by securing the thread with a backstitch tack.

prickstitch

The prickstitch is a variation of the backstitch and is used most often for inserting a hand-picked zipper. For details about the hand-picked technique, see Zippers, page 147.

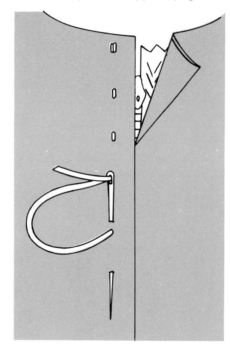

Backstitch tack to attach the thread to the fabric.

Take a very small stitch behind the thread, through all fabric layers.

Bring the needle to the topside about ¼″ (6 mm) ahead of your stitch.

Continue the stitches along the stitching line, forming short stitches on the topside about ¼″ (6 mm) apart.

Finish by pulling the thread to the underside and securing it with a backstitch tack.

overcast stitch

This is a seam finish to prevent raw edges from raveling.

Backstitch tack to attach the thread to the fabric.

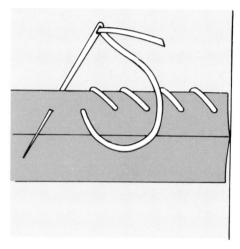

Take a diagonal stitch over the edge of the fabric and continue stitching evenly and at a uniform depth.

Finish by securing the thread with a backstitch tack.

thread chain

The thread chain is a continuous series of looped stitches that form a chain. It is most often used for belt carriers or for thread eyes used with hooks. You will need to mark the location of the thread chain on your fabric.

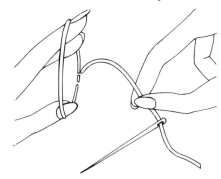

Backstitch tack to attach the thread to the fabric where the thread chain begins.

Take a small stitch at the marking and pull the thread through, leaving a loop.

Spread the loop and hold it open with your thumb and index finger.

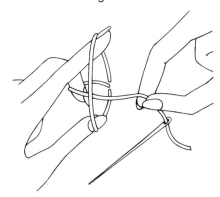

Reach through the loop with your middle finger and catch the long end of the thread to form a new loop.

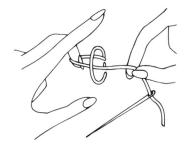

Pull the new loop through the first loop to let the first loop slide off your fingers.

Pull both the new loop and the thread so that the first loop becomes smaller and forms a knot at the base of the thread chain.

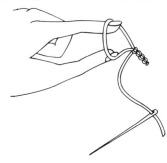

Keep forming new loops and sliding the previous loop down the thread evenly, close to the last knot.

Continue until you have the thread chain the desired length.

Secure by slipping the needle and thread through the last loop and stitching into the fabric.

Finish by making a backstitch tack on the underside of the fabric.

whipstitch

Versatile, and easy too, the whipstitch is a handy stitch to know for finishing up dozens of small sewing jobs. Keep it in mind for applying such things as belt carriers or fasteners, and for finishing some quick and easy hems.

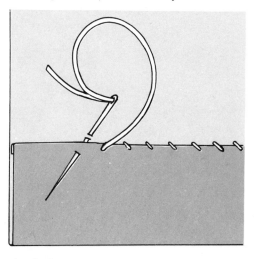

Backstitch tack to attach the thread to the topside of the fabric.

Take small, even stitches, catching both fabric edges with one stitch.

- Pick up only one or two threads of the fabric as you sew.

- Stitches should extend over the edges at regular intervals.

Finish by securing the thread with a backstitch tack.

hems

A hem is a finish for the bottom edge of a sleeve, skirt or pants leg. Hems are, of course, influenced by the rise and fall of fashion trends.

To decide how long or short your hem should be, consider the fabric and style of the garment you are making. Above all, choose the hem length which flatters you most.

Generally, hems are made by simply turning the raw edge of fabric toward the inside of the garment and attaching this edge so that the hemline hangs evenly and does not seem obvious as the garment is worn. Sometimes, however, hems are faced, bound or finished with a decorative technique to add design interest to a garment.

In this section you'll learn the fine art of hemming in a variety of ways.

MARKING THE HEMLINE

The first step toward completing a hem is marking the hemline. Check your pattern to see how much hem allowance has been provided.

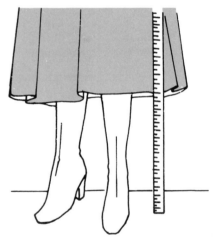

Try on the garment.

- It's best to mark the hemline while you are wearing the same undergarments and shoes you will wear when you actually use the garment.

Measure from the floor and mark the hemline with pins or tailor's chalk an equal distance all around.

- You'll need someone to help you mark the hem correctly.

Turn the hem along the markings and pin in place.

Adjust the hem if necessary to be sure it falls evenly and that the length is attractive.

- Note that bias or circular garments must hang for a full day before hemming since they often sag unevenly.

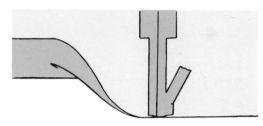

Turn the hem along the markings and pin or hand baste in place.

- Reduce bulk at seams by trimming any seam allowances that fall within the hem.

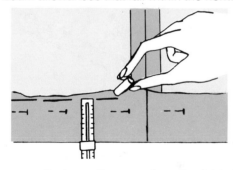

Measure the hem allowance from the folded edge using a hem gauge or small ruler.

Mark and trim the hem allowance to an equal width all around.

Finish the hem using any one of the following methods. Choose a method suitable for your fabric and garment.

plain hem

A plain hem is used primarily on straight and slightly shaped edges. Allow a 2″-3″ (50-75 mm) hem allowance.

Finish the raw edge.

- Refer to Seam Finishes, page 121.

- Use seam tape if you want to conceal the cut edge of the hem. Preshrink the seam tape first. Wet it thoroughly and then press it with a steam iron to dry it completely. With regular machine stitching, sew one side of the seam tape to the cut edge of the hem. Fold the overlapping edge of the seam tape under for a smooth finish.

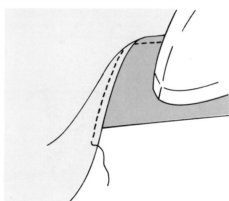

Turn the hem allowance under and press.

Hem with a blindstitch, catchstitch, slipstitch or a whipstitch.

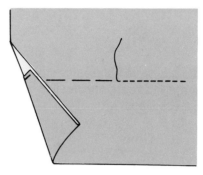

- For an interesting finish, you can topstitch the hem in place with matching or contrasting thread. Use a straight, zigzag or decorative stitch.

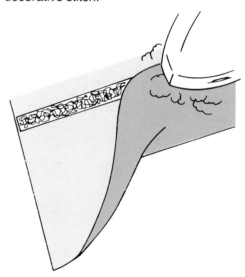

Or, you can fuse your hem instead of stitching it by following these steps.

Place a narrow strip of fusible web between the garment and the hem just below the edge of the hem.

- Refer to Fusing, page 17.

Press to fuse, following the manufacturer's directions accurately.

hem for a pleated garment

Pleated garments with seams crossing the hemline will have a smoother finish if you follow these steps.

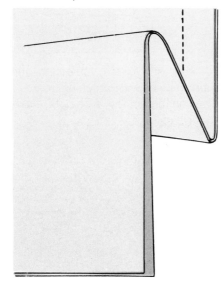

Stitch the seam to about 8″ (20.5 cm) from the hem edge.

Complete the hem, following the instructions for a Plain Hem, page 83.

■ Note that each garment section will be hemmed separately.

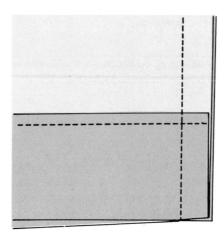

Follow these steps to complete the garment seams.

Stitch seam allowances together through all layers of the hem.

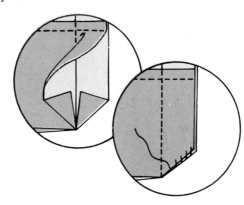

Fold the bottom edges of the seam allowances up diagonally as illustrated.

Whipstitch folded edges together.

Press garment seam allowances as the pattern guidesheet suggests.

For more information, see Pleats, page 100.

narrow hem

The narrow hem is a quick, easy and clean finished hem made by machine. Allow a ⅝″ (15 mm) hem allowance.

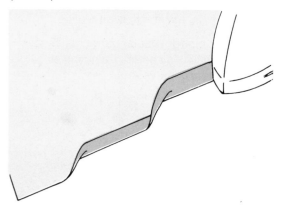

Turn the raw edge under ⅝″ (15 mm) and press.

Edgestitch all around.

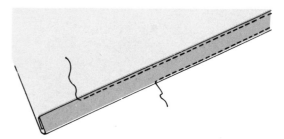

Tuck under the raw edge and press.

Topstitch all around.

shaped hem

The shaped hem is used on flared or circular garments with a curved hem edge. Allow approximately 1″ (25 mm) hem allowance.

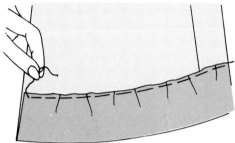

Stitch ¼″ (6 mm) from the raw edge using machine basting, about 6-8 stitches per inch (every 25 mm).

Match seamlines and pull up the threads to ease in any excess fullness.

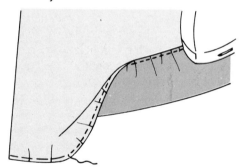

Turn the hem allowance under.

Press the hem allowance to shrink out excess fullness.

Finish the raw edge.

■ Refer to Seam Finishes, page 121, for more information.

Hem by hand, using the blindstitch for the best results.

rolled hem

The rolled hem is a very narrow hem, used mainly for lightweight and sheer fabrics.

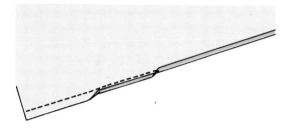

Stitch about ¼″ (6 mm) away from the raw edge.

Roll the edge under twice to enclose the raw edge.

■ You can anchor one end with a pin to an armchair for more control as you roll the hem.

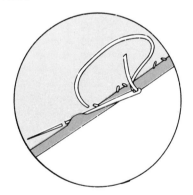

Slipstitch the rolled edge to the garment.

easy, interesting hems

Make the most of your hems. Decide whether your fabric or garment would look better if you used a new idea.

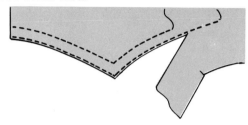

First, try a hem that isn't a hem. With natural or synthetic leathers and suedes, try the "no-hem" hem. Just cut the edge and leave it raw. For a decorative finish, topstitch and edgestitch.

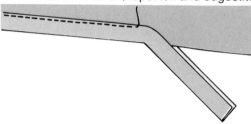

Or, try binding the hem edge of your garment with a matching or contrasting binding. Refer to Bindings, page 36, for more information.

You can also use a narrow stitch for a nice, narrow hem on knits.

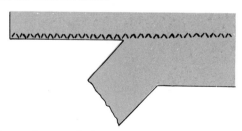

Use a zigzag stitch along the hemline through a single thickness of fabric. Then trim away the excess fabric close to the stitches.

interfacing

Interfacing is the inside story of fashion.

There are many types of interfacing but all of them are designed to be used undercover.

Interfacing fabrics are attached to garment areas such as the collar, lapel, pocket and front or back openings; they are placed in between the outer fabric and the facing to provide extra support and help shape the garment.

types of interfacing

Interfacing fabrics can be woven or nonwoven and can be made from a variety of fibers. Several degrees of crispness are available, from soft through firm, to satisfy any sewing requirement.

Some types of interfacing are fusible and can be attached to the garment by pressing with a steam iron. Other interfacings must be stitched in position.

Always select an interfacing which requires the same type of care as the finished garment. It just wouldn't do, for example, to put a "dry clean only" interfacing in a "machine wash, tumble dry" garment.

Choose an interfacing that compliments your garment as well. The interfacing should have enough weight to support and help shape, but not distort, the fabric. Imagine a very sturdy interfacing in a sheer chiffon collar. You'd lose the soft elegance of the fabric. Instead, a softer interfacing would help accent the flowing beauty of the chiffon.

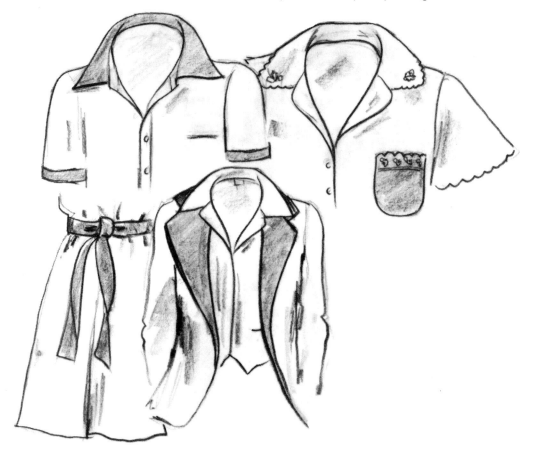

- Woven interfacings work best with woven fabrics. Some woven interfacings, such as hair canvas, are made with natural fibers. These are especially good for shaping and molding natural fabrics such as woolens. As a rule, woven interfacings are a bit too rigid for knits because they don't have the necessary flexibility for such stretchable fabrics. Although it is possible to use woven interfacings which are cut on the bias for certain knits, generally nonwoven interfacings are recommended.

- Nonwoven interfacings are available in three types: all-bias, crosswise stretch and nonstretchable. All-bias nonwoven interfacing provides the greatest amount of stretch in all directions. Crosswise stretch nonwoven interfacing has the most stretch horizontally, which makes it an excellent choice for many knits. Non-stretchable interfacing is not used for garments since it provides no stretch. However, this interfacing is handy for craft and home decorating projects.

FUSIBLE INTERFACING METHOD

Woven or nonwoven fusible interfacing has a heat-sensitive adhesive on one side. The heat, steam and pressure of an iron will melt the adhesive to join the interfacing to your fabric.

Follow manufacturer's directions for use since each brand requires slightly different techniques for successful, permanent bonding. Before you begin, always test a small piece of the interfacing by attaching it to a fabric scrap to be sure the results are what you expect. For more information on Fusing, see page 17.

Here are some general guidelines for using fusible interfacing.

Cut the interfacing pieces following the directions on your pattern guidesheet.

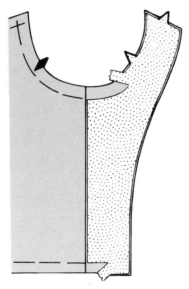

Trim away all seam allowances—they aren't needed when you can fuse the interfacing directly to the fabric.

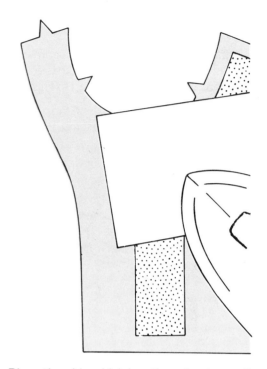

Place the side which has the adhesive on the wrong side of your garment, matching the cut edges of the interfacing to the seamlines of the garment.

Fuse the interfacing in position, following the manufacturer's instructions.

- Fusible interfacing may leave a ridge at the cut edge where the interfacing extends into the body of the garment. Test the interfacing on a scrap of your fabric. If it leaves a ridge, fuse the interfacing to the facing rather than to the garment.

SEW-IN METHOD

Sew-in interfacings are applied to the garment by hand or machine basting. Follow these simple steps to do it right, from start to finish.

Cut the interfacing pieces following the directions on your pattern guidesheet.

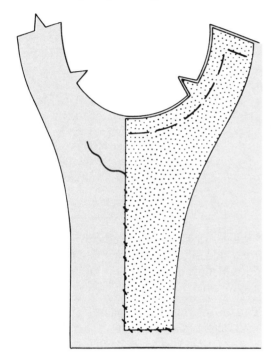

Baste the interfacing to the wrong side of the garment by hand or machine next to the seamline, just into the seam allowance.

- If you're machine basting, it is extremely important to stitch directionally. For more information about directional stitching, see page 93.

- If you're hand basting, whipstitch along any folded edges such as a front or back opening. Be careful to catch only a few fabric threads to prevent the stitching from showing on the right side.

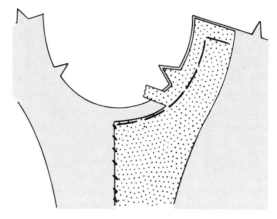

Trim the seam allowances close to the stitching.

machine stitching

Your sewing machine probably can do more than you think.

As you start sewing, it's important to learn all you can about your machine so that you will be able to use it well to make a wide variety of garments, accessories or decorative projects.

There are many different types and brands of sewing machines. Each has special qualities and care requirements. Study the booklet which comes with your machine to understand how it operates and what it can do for you.

cleaning your sewing machine

A sewing machine will operate best for a long time if you take good care of it. Like any other piece of machinery, it must be cleaned often and some machines require occasional oiling. For exact instructions, refer to your sewing machine booklet and follow these general procedures.

- Clean your machine thoroughly after you have completed a garment. Use a small brush to remove lint which has accumulated around the bobbin or other areas. A machine that is not being used regularly should be cleaned at least twice a year. Oil the machine carefully as the manufacturer recommends.

- Keep a lint brush handy for in-between cleaning. This is especially important when you are working on linty fabrics such as corduroy or fuzzy woolens.

- Cover your machine when it is not in use to protect it from dust buildup.

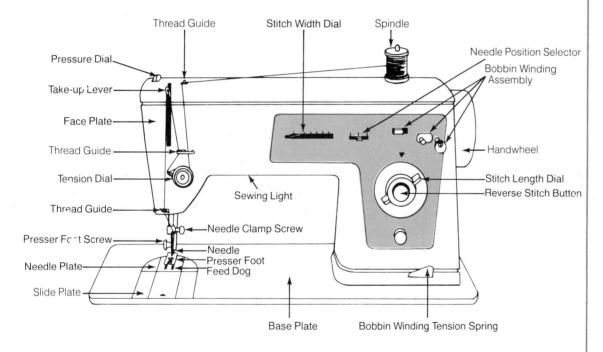

Thread Guide · Stitch Width Dial · Spindle · Needle Position Selector · Bobbin Winding Assembly · Pressure Dial · Take-up Lever · Face Plate · Thread Guide · Tension Dial · Sewing Light · Handwheel · Thread Guide · Stitch Length Dial · Reverse Stitch Button · Needle Clamp Screw · Presser Foot Screw · Needle · Presser Foot · Feed Dog · Needle Plate · Slide Plate · Base Plate · Bobbin Winding Tension Spring

needles

There are several different sizes and types of sewing machine needles, each designed for a specific purpose.

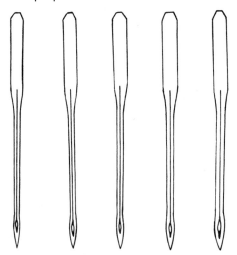

In the American coding system, needle sizes range from 9 to 18. The higher the number, the thicker the needle.

Choose a needle suited to the type and weight of your fabric. A size 9 or 11 needle is ideal for fine lightweight fabrics such as chiffon, crepe de Chine or voile. A size 14 needle is useful for medium weight fabrics including muslin, corduroy and flannel. The heavier size 16 needle is best for sturdy or thick fabrics such as burlap, sailcloth or heavy coating.

Some foreign manufacturers use a different numbering system for needles, but the basic rule still applies. The lighter and finer the fabric, the finer the needle should be.

Each needle size is available in several types or styles. These types are based generally on the design of the needle point.

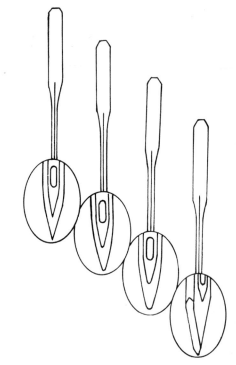

- Needles with sharp points are recommended for all woven fabrics, especially fine ones such as organdy, chiffon or gabardine.

- All-purpose needles are slightly blunter than those which are labeled "sharp" but they still have a definite point; these are useful for most woven and knitted fabrics.

- Ball-point needles have a rounded tip and are suited only for knits. Their purpose is to separate rather than pierce the fibers of the fabric during stitching. Piercing the fibers could cause snagging.

- Wedge-point needles are designed to penetrate leathers and vinyls without splitting or cracking them.

Many stitching problems are caused by the needle. The following facts will help you understand how a needle can make the difference in your sewing.

1. A needle that is inserted incorrectly will cause skipped stitches, or it will not stitch at all. The flat side of the needle must be placed in a specific direction. Refer to your sewing machine booklet for information about how to insert the needle correctly.

2. The wrong size needle for the machine or the fabric will affect the stitch formation. A thick needle on a fine fabric will cause the thread to split and fray.

3. Dull or damaged needles cause a multitude of problems, including unbalanced or skipped stitches. A needle should be changed after every eight hours of sewing, approximately after every garment you make. Throw out all your old needles before you ruin your fabric with them. A blunt needle will make a thumping noise as it penetrates the fabric, or it may cause skipped stitches.

4. The finishes on fabric can produce a buildup of residue on the needle, resulting in skipped stitches. Clean the needle with oil, detergent or a cleaning solvent.

thread

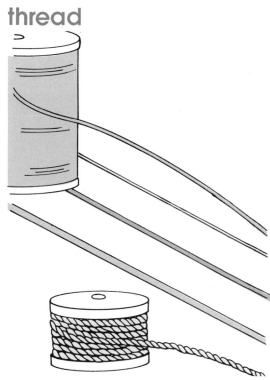

A good all-purpose polyester or polyester/cotton thread is the best choice for almost all of your sewing needs. These threads are strong, flexible and available in a wide range of colors.

Polyester or polyester/cotton threads are recommended especially for knits since they are able to stretch slightly. This provides a sturdy seam which will not break as the garment is worn.

Choose a thread whose color matches your fabric. If the exact shade isn't available, select a thread which is slightly darker than the fabric. As you stitch your seams, the color of the thread will blend nicely. Plaids and prints should be stitched with a thread closest to the dominant color of the fabric.

There are also specialty threads, such as silk, cotton, heavy-duty or buttonhole twist which may be useful for certain sewing purposes.

- Silk threads are very fine and quite strong. They are excellent for basting delicate fabrics which may be marked by other types of basting thread. In addition, silk thread is sometimes recommended for sewing on fine fabrics made from the natural fibers of silk or wool.

- Cotton thread used to be the most common type and is still a good choice for most woven fabrics, especially those made of cotton or silk, such as gingham, percale, voile or satin. Today cotton thread is not available in many stores since polyester or polyester/cotton thread is considered more useful for more purposes.

- Heavy-duty thread is extra thick and strong. It is a wise choice for projects such as upholstering which require strength and durability.

- Buttonhole twist is a shiny thick thread recommended for topstitching or similar decorative uses. It is available in silk or polyester.

pressure and feed

- Pressure is the downward force applied on the fabric as it moves under the presser foot.

- Feed is the upward force that moves the fabric under the presser foot.

- Pressure and feed interact to produce an evenly stitched seam.

The pressure and feed on your machine can be adjusted so that the fabric layers move evenly with one another. Refer to your sewing machine booklet to find your pressure regulator. Most machines have a dial, a push bar or a screw regulator. Some of the newer machine models include an automatic pressure regulator and do not need to be adjusted manually.

Basically, light pressure is used for lightweight fabrics and heavy pressure for heavyweight fabrics. The correct amount of pressure will produce seams which are stitched evenly. Too much pressure will cause the top layer to slip while the bottom layer gathers up.

Uneven or skipped stitches and poor control of the fabric layers result when too little pressure is used.

The purpose of the feed is to move the fabric into position for each stitch. The distance the fabric moves is controlled by the stitch length regulator.

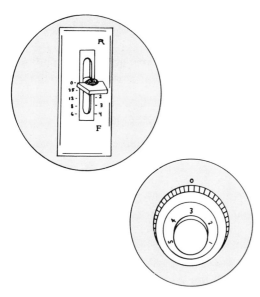

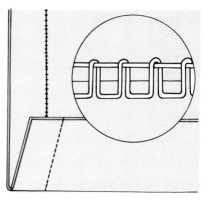

The numbers on the regulator are based on either the inch or the metric measurement. If the numbers on your stitch regulator run from 6 to 20, it indicates the number of stitches per inch (each 25 mm).

Those machines numbered 0 to 4 indicate the actual length of the stitch in millimeters. A recommended stitch length of 12 stitches to the inch is equivalent to a stitch length of 2.1 mm.

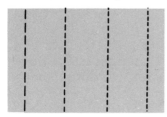

You can adjust the stitch length regulator to your specific sewing needs. Most seams are stitched at 12-15 stitches to the inch (25 mm), or a stitch length of 2-2.5 mm.

Reinforced stitches are smaller, easing or basting stitches are longer.

tension

Tension is the pressure that controls the amount of thread fed into each stitch. When the tension is adjusted properly, the stitches will be well balanced. That is, the stitches will look the same on the top and bottom of the fabric.

Every machine has a top thread tension control and most have a bobbin tension control. These controls increase or decrease the pressure on the threads as they are fed through the machine. If it is necessary to adjust the tension, do so by using the top tension control. Bobbin tensions are set at the factory and should not be adjusted unless absolutely necessary. Your sewing machine booklet will show you how. Many newer sewing machines have devices which adjust the top and bottom tension automatically.

Top tensions are controlled by a numbered dial. Basically, the higher the number, the tighter the tension.

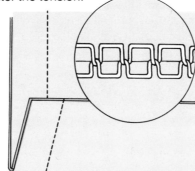

■ Correct tension: The stitch is balanced on both sides of the fabric. The link is formed right in the middle of the fabric layers. Equal amounts of thread from the top and the bottom have been fed into the stitch and therefore no loops appear on either side.

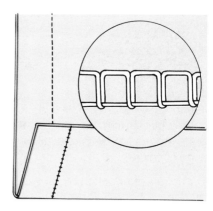

■ Tight top tension: Loops will form on the top of the fabric if there is not enough thread being fed from the top to meet the bobbin thread in the middle of the fabric layers. Decrease or loosen the top tension to form a balanced stitch.

■ Loose top tension: Loops will form on the bottom of the fabric. Too much thread is being fed into each stitch from the top. Increase or tighten the top tension to form a balanced stitch.

SEAMS

Seams are the sections of a garment or other item where two or more layers of fabric are joined by stitches. There are a few basic facts you should know about seams to make your sewing a success.

directional stitching

Directional stitching is the technique of stitching with the grain of the fabric to prevent stretching or changing the shape of the seam area. It is easy to determine which direction is with the grain by running your finger along the cut fabric edge. One direction feels smooth; running your finger in the other direction feels rough and pulls up the threads. The direction that feels smooth is with the grain. Basically, if you stitch from the wide part of a fabric section to the narrow part, you will be stitching with the grain.

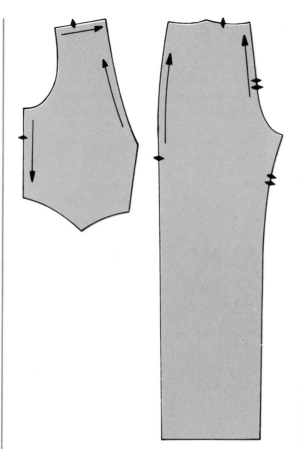

On long, shaped seams where the direction of the grain changes, stitch in the direction that stays with the grain longest. Necklines, for example, change grain direction. Because of this, they should be stitched from the shoulder seams to the center front or center back. Straight grain seams can be stitched in either direction.

seam guides

Seam allowances are marked on your pattern tissue. Usually seam allowances are ⅝" (15 mm) wide, measuring from the cut edge. As you sew, it's important to keep the seam allowances the exact width they are supposed to be. That way the fabric sections will come together evenly and the garment will fit correctly.

The best way to keep seam allowances even is to match up the cut edges with a marking on your sewing machine. Then watch the cut edges, not the needle, as the fabric moves through the machine.

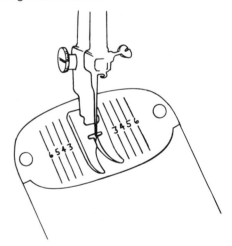

Seam guidelines are marked on the needleplate of many machines. The numbered lines indicate eighths of an inch (3 mm) from the needle. Some machines also include a crossline at ⅝" (15 mm) which acts as a guide for pivoting corners.

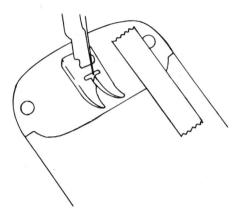

It's easy to make a mark on your machine if seam guides are not already on your needleplate. Just measure ⅝" (15 mm) to the right of the needle and place a piece of cellophane or plastic tape lengthwise on the needleplate.

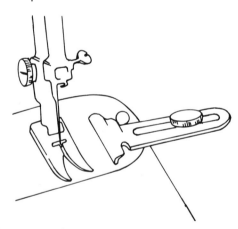

You may prefer to use a seam gauge attachment as a guide. It is especially helpful for stitching curves. If your machine does not include a seam gauge that screws onto the base plate of the machine, you can buy a magnetic one that works on all machines.

stitching a seam

Using a machine to sew a seam is easy and fast, if you know how to use the machine correctly. Begin the right way by learning methods that work every time.

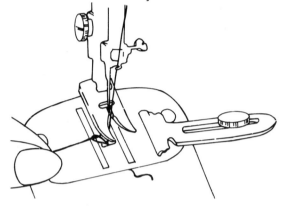

Raise the presser foot and thread the machine.

Hold the end of the thread, turn the hand wheel toward you to pull up the bobbin thread and raise the needle to its highest point.

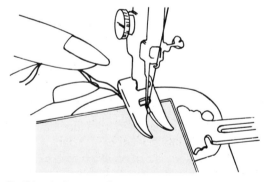

Pull both the needle and bobbin threads under the presser foot and behind the machine.

Place the fabric under the presser foot about ½" (13 mm) in from the beginning of the stitching line.

Match the cut edge to the seamline marking or seam gauge attachment on your machine.

■ The bulk of the fabric will be to the left of the machine needle.

Hold the threads with your index finger and lower the needle into the fabric by turning the hand wheel toward you.

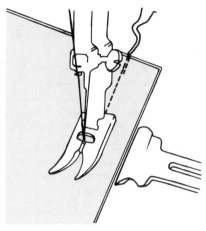

Lower the presser foot.

Backstitch to the edge of the fabric, reverse the stitching direction and stitch forward along the seamline.

■ Hold the threads until you have taken the first few stitches to prevent them from jamming into the bobbin.

■ This entire stitching procedure should be done smoothly in one operation. There is no need to stop and start as you reverse stitching directions. As you gain confidence in using the machine, your sewing habits will become smooth and even.

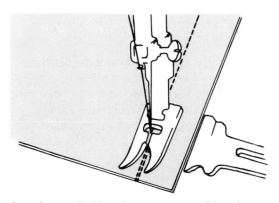

Continue stitching the seam, matching the cut edge of the fabric to the seamline marking or seam gauge attachment.

Reinforce the end of the seam by backstitching a few stitches.

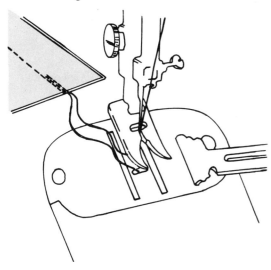

Raise the presser foot and pull the fabric and threads back and away from the needle area.

Clip the threads close to the fabric.

easestitching

The easestitch is a moderately long stitch used to pull in slight fullness evenly, without causing tucks or gathers. It is used in areas such as the shoulder and the waistline.

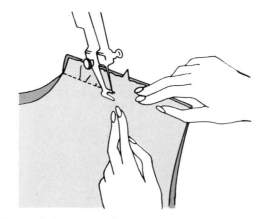

Easestitching can often be done in one step. Just stitch your seam using a regular stitch length. Place the larger garment section on top. Gently ease in excess fullness as you stitch so that the notches and other markings match. If you are working with a fabric which is difficult to ease, follow these steps.

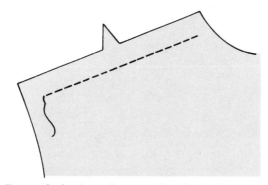

Easestitch along the seamline through a single thickness of fabric, using about 8-10 stitches per inch (every 25 mm).

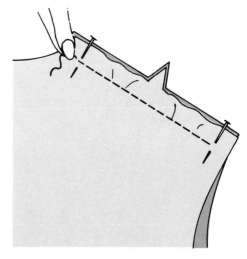

Match the markings at the eased area to the markings on the other garment section.

Pull the bobbin thread to ease in the fullness on the fabric until the markings on your garment sections match.

Stitch the sections together along the seamline.

staystitching

The staystitch is used to prevent stretching at corners or very curved areas, such as necklines and armholes, on loosely woven or stretch fabrics. It is also used to reinforce an area before clipping.

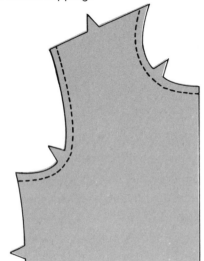

Staystitch about ⅛" (3 mm) away from the seamline toward the cut edge of the seam allowance using a regular stitch length.

- Stitch directionally through a single thickness of fabric. Refer to Machine Stitching, page 93.
- Be careful not to stretch the garment as you sew.

Check your garment against the pattern tissue for any changes in the shape of the area you just staystitched.

Adjust, if the garment has stretched, by pulling the thread.

- If you have too much ease, pop the threads to release the staystitching.

stitch-in-the-ditch

This is a stitch done from the right side of the garment in the ridge of another seam. It is used primarily to hold a bottom layer of fabric, such as a facing, waistband or binding, in position.

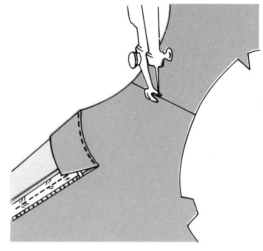

Stitch, using a regular stitch length and matching thread, in the ridge of the seam, through all thicknesses.

topstitching

Topstitching is used mainly as a decorative or trim stitch on the right side of the garment. It is usually a long stitch, sewn with either matching or contrasting thread. You can use a single or double strand of regular sewing thread or buttonhole twist.

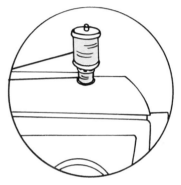

If you're using a double strand of regular thread, thread your machine as usual but use two spools of thread. If you don't have two spool pins, wind an extra bobbin and place it under the thread spool.

Buttonhole twist is thicker than thread. Therefore, if you use buttonhole twist, you should switch to a larger needle to prevent the thread from splitting.

Set your machine to the stitch length you want.

- Topstitching usually is longer than regular machine stitching, about 6-8 stitches per inch (every 25 mm).

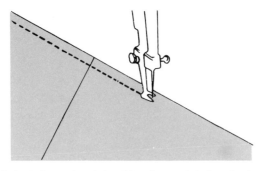

Stitch from the right side of your fabric, placing the presser foot next to a seam or fabric edge for a guide.

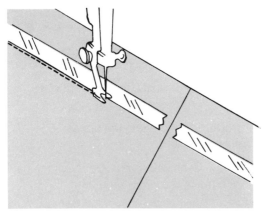

■ You can use a special sewing tape available in notions stores, as a guide for stitching. Just place the tape along the topstitching line and stitch next to it. Do not stitch through the tape or you will pull the stitches loose when you remove the tape from the fabric.

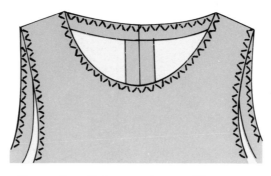

■ Decorative stitches can be used for topstitching. A zigzag stitch looks great on T-shirts and other sportswear.

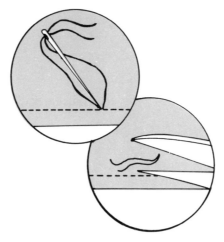

■ If you run out of thread at a noticeable place, just rethread your machine and continue stitching at the exact spot. Leave thread ends long enough so they can be brought to the wrong side of the garment using a hand needle. Tie thread ends to secure them.

understitching

Understitching is a line of straight stitches sewn to prevent the bottom layer of fabric from rolling out. This technique is used for facings, lapels and similar areas.

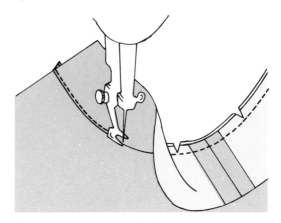

Press the trimmed and clipped seam allowances toward the facing or under the layer of fabric.

Stitch with a regular stitch length, from the right side, close to the seamline, through the fabric and seam allowances.

corners and curves

It's a cinch to stitch perfect corners and curves if you follow these simple steps.

PIVOTING A CORNER

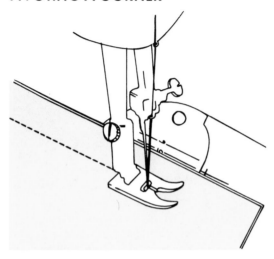

Match the cut edge of the fabric to the seamline marking or the seam gauge attachment on your machine.

Stitch the seam to the corner where the seamlines cross and leave the needle in the fabric.

- Shorten the stitch length around the corner for reinforcement.

- The guideline of your needleplate will show you where to stop. Measure the distance from the needle to the edge of the fabric if you don't have a crossline marking. Stop sewing at ⅝″ (15 mm) to pivot the corner.

- If you are stitching an area where you can't see the seam gauge, such as a pocket in a seam, mark the point that is ⅝″ (15 mm) from the corner and stitch to the mark.

Raise the presser foot and pivot the fabric on the needle.

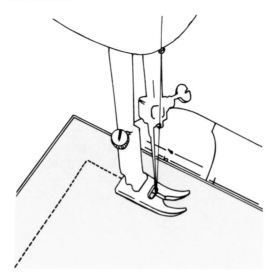

Lower the presser foot and continue stitching.

BLUNTING THE CORNER

This is an extra trick for achieving sharp pointed corners on collars, cuffs, lapels or any other enclosed corner seam. The diagonal stitch allows a bit more room in the corner, thus preventing all the seam allowances from bunching up inside the point.

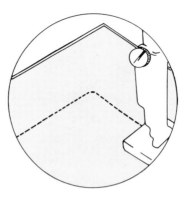

Stitch to the corner where the seamlines cross.

- Shorten the stitch length around the corner for reinforcement.

Make one diagonal stitch across the corner.

- You can make two if your fabric is heavy or bulky.

Continue stitching along the opposite seamline.

- Use your hand wheel to guide the machine as you make the diagonal stitch.

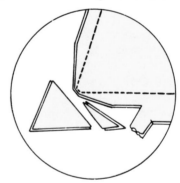

Trim the seam allowances close to the stitching on both sides of the turned corner.

Turn the fabric right side out, using a pin or needle to pull out the point completely.

pleats

Pleats are fabric folds that provide controlled fullness. They can be formed on either the right or wrong side of the fabric, depending on the design of the garment.

Some pleats fall in soft folds and others are pressed sharp along the edges. Regardless of the type of pleat you're making, it's important to mark accurately and follow your guidesheet carefully for specific instructions.

This general information will help you complete your pleats with speed and perfection.

making pleats

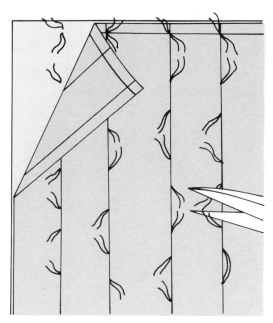

Mark the foldlines and placement lines with tailor tacks.

- Simply take small stitches every 3″ (75 mm) through the pattern tissue and fabric. Clip the thread between stitches.

- Use one color thread for the foldline and another color for the placement line.

Refer to Marking, page 13, for more information.

Remove the pattern tissue carefully, to avoid pulling out your thread markings.

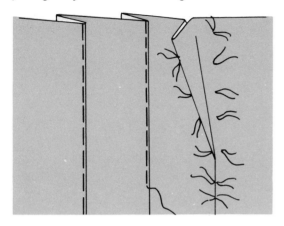

Baste each pleat in place along the entire foldline.

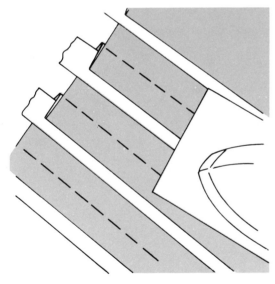

Press the pleats carefully, using a presscloth.

- Place strips of paper under the foldlines to prevent pressmark ridges along the placement lines.

- For soft pleats, press lightly.

- For extra sharp pleats, use a damp presscloth and allow the pleats to dry thoroughly before removing the garment from the ironing table.

- For a more permanent crease, you can have your pleats pressed professionally.

Complete your pleats according to the guidesheet instructions.

Reduce bulk at seams crossing the hem allowance by following these simple steps, or refer to Hems, page 82.

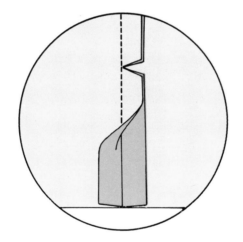

1. Clip the seam above the hem area.

2. Press the seam open below the clip.

3. Trim the seam allowances below the clip to reduce bulk.

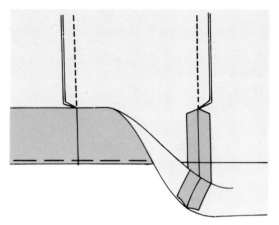

4. Complete the hem.

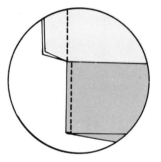

5. Fold the pleat, right sides together, with the seam on the edge of the fold.

6. Edgestitch through all thicknesses.

topstitching pleats

Topstitching is not only a decorative finish but also a valuable technique for holding pleats in place and helping them hang smoothly. It is normally done in the waist-to-hip area through all thicknesses of fabric.

Mark each pleat with a pin to indicate where the topstitching will end.

Topstitch through all thicknesses, with the garment right side up, starting at the pin and stitching to the top of the pleat.

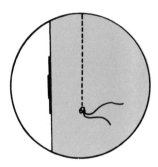

Pull threads to the underside and tie.

edgestitching pleats

Edgestitching is done along the fold of a pleat to give it a sharper crease. Always stitch from the bottom to the top after the hem is complete.

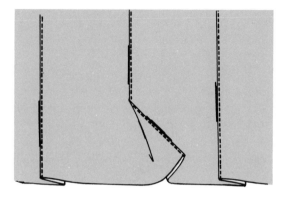

Press the pleat carefully along the foldline.

Edgestitch along the fold from the bottom of the pleat to the top.

pockets

Pockets are pretty and practical.

The four basic types are the Patch Pocket, the In-Seam Pocket, the Front Hip Pocket and the Welt Pocket. Some garments have more than one type, so you're smart to learn the basic techniques for making all of them. Then you'll be prepared to put pockets in place correctly, every time.

Rely on your pattern guidesheet for exact instructions on making pockets for a particular garment. These general guidelines will help you as you sew.

Remember, pockets are one of the most obvious items on a garment. The time you spend on them will pay off in pockets that show your excellence and workmanship.

patch pockets

Patch pockets are made from fabric pieces which are stitched on top of the garment, by hand or machine. When you're working with a print or plaid that requires matching, be sure to cut your pockets to match your garment. If you prefer, you can cut the pockets on the bias for contrast and an interesting design detail.

If your garment has a pair of pockets, be sure that the finished pockets are identical before you sew them to the garment.

UNLINED PATCH POCKETS

For sharp corners without bulk, follow these steps carefully.

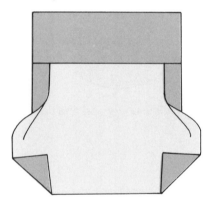

Press corners at the bottom of the pocket diagonally to the wrong side.

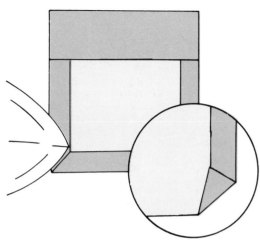

Fold the edges to the wrong side along the seamline, forming a miter at the corner.

Press the edges in place, forming sharp pointed corners.

For smooth rounded curves without puckers and points, follow these steps.

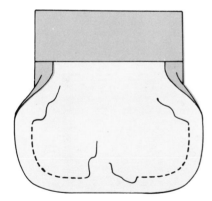

Stitch around the curve next to the seamline, in the seam allowance, using about 8-10 stitches per inch (each 25 mm).

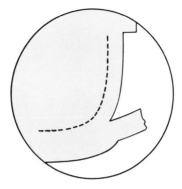

Trim the seam allowance to about ¼″ (6 mm) from the stitching line.

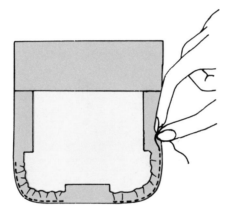

Pull up the stitches around the curves, just enough to draw in the seam allowance and shape the pocket curve.

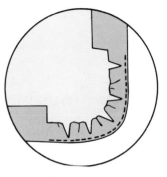

Notch the seam allowance if necessary to reduce pressure and avoid puckers.

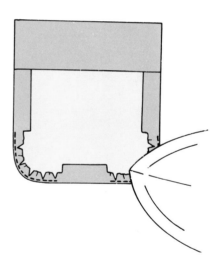

Press the pocket, forming smooth, evenly rounded curves.

LINED PATCH POCKETS

As a rule, patch pockets are unlined and are designed to have a foldover facing along the top edge.

You may want to adapt the pattern piece for a patch pocket by lining it with a lighter weight fabric. Follow these steps to make a patch pocket which is lined to the edge.

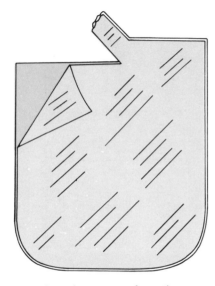

Cut two pocket pieces, one from the garment fabric and another from the lining fabric, using the original pattern piece.

■ Consider the top edge foldline on the pattern piece as the top seamline of your lined pocket.

Trim the garment and lining fabric to form a ⅝" (15 mm) seam allowance above the original foldline of the top pocket edge.

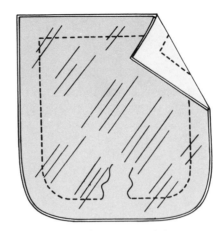

Stitch the lining to the pocket, right sides together, leaving a small opening along one edge for turning.

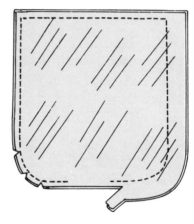

Trim the seam allowances and notch around the curves or corners as necessary.

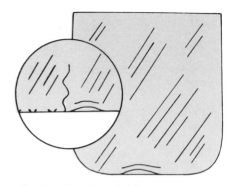

Turn the lined pocket right side out.

Slipstitch the opening closed.

Press the pocket, making sure there is no lining showing on the right side along the pocket edges.

APPLYING PATCH POCKETS

Baste the pocket to the garment by hand along the placement markings.

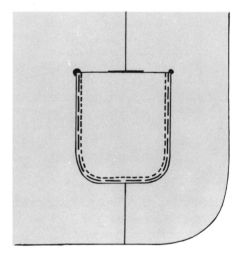

Stitch the pocket to the garment by topstitching or edgestitching.

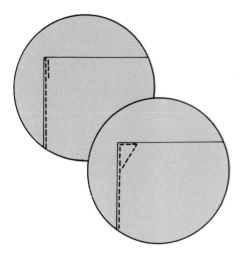

Reinforce the open corners of the pocket by machine backstitching.

■ You can also reinforce the open corners with more decorative stitching, such as a triangular shape.

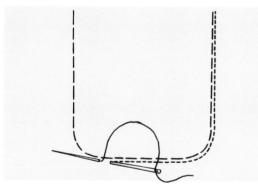

■ If you prefer not to topstitch, you can apply the pocket by hand with a strong backstitch on the wrong side of the garment.

pockets in a seam

Some pockets are enclosed in a seam and cannot be seen when the garment is worn. Other pockets which are enclosed in a seam are designed as a fashion detail and are topstitched on the right side of the garment.

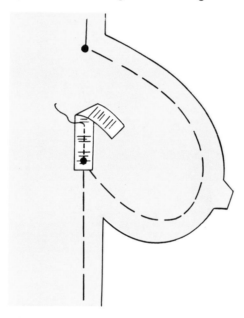

■ To prevent stretching along the pocket edge, reinforce the foldline with seam tape.

■ If heavyweight fabrics are recommended, a separate pocket extension is included with the pattern. Cut the pocket extension from a lightweight lining fabric to reduce bulk.

■ Mark the stitching line around the top and bottom of the pocket.

APPLYING POCKETS IN A SEAM

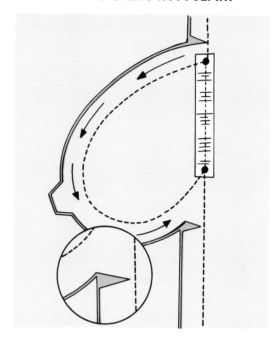

Stitch the garment seams together following the markings around the pocket area.

■ Use shorter stitches near the corners to give them extra strength.

Clip the seam allowance on the back side of the garment at the top and bottom of the pocket.

■ As always, clip to, but not through, the stitching.

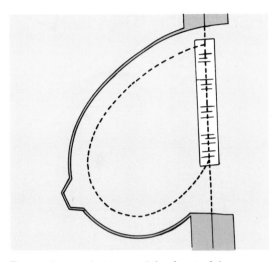

Press the pocket toward the front of the garment.

Topstitch the pocket on the garment front for a decorative finish.

For a smooth, even topstitching line, follow these steps.

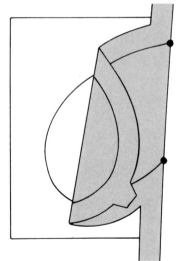

1. Transfer the stitching line from the pattern tissue to a piece of paper.

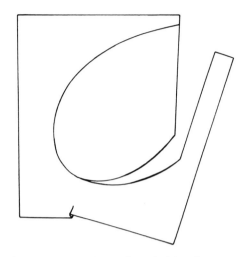

2. Cut the paper along the stitching line markings.

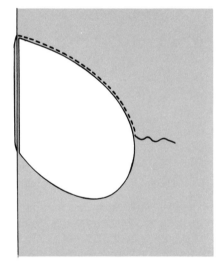

3. Place the paper on the garment with the cut edge where the stitching line should be.

4. Topstitch the pocket to the garment front along the cut edge of the paper through all thicknesses.

front hip pocket

Front hip pockets are angular or curved pockets on the garment front of pants and skirts. They are attached to the waist and side seams of the garment.

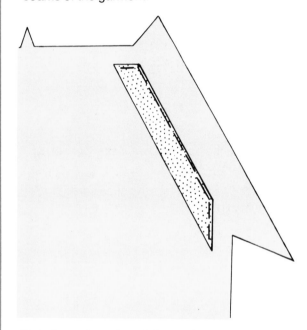

Reinforce the edge of the pocket with interfacing or seam tape to prevent stretching.

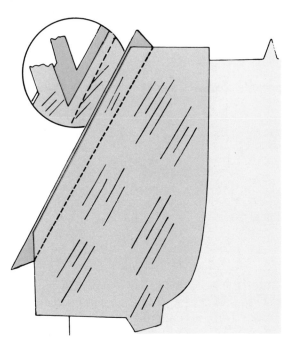

Cut the pocket lining from a lightweight fabric.

Stitch the pocket lining to the garment extension.

Trim the seam allowances, notching curved edges as necessary.

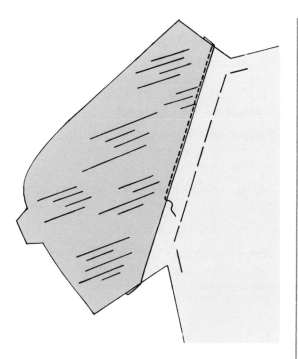

Understitch the seam allowances to the pocket lining or pocket facing.

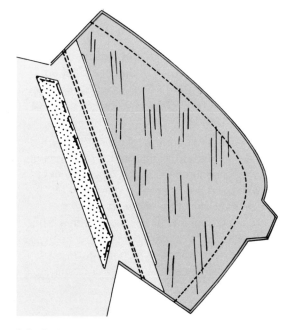

Stitch the pocket to the pocket lining.

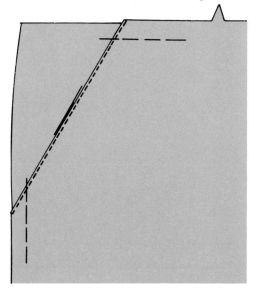

Baste the pocket to the garment along the seamlines.

welt pockets

Welt pockets are inside pockets made with welting on one or both sides of a slashed opening in the garment. A welt pocket may be finished with a single or double welt, with or without a pocket flap.

Welt pockets are made following somewhat the same method as for a bound buttonhole. Your success in making this type of pocket depends on precise marking for pocket placement, accurate stitching and very careful cutting! If you're working with a fabric that requires matching, cut your pocket welts and flaps so they will match the garment.

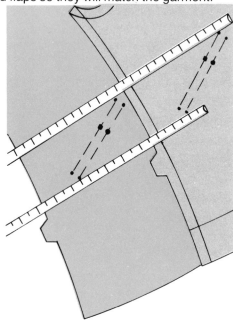

Transfer pocket markings from the pattern piece to your pocket and the right side of your garment.

■ Refer to Marking, page 13, for more information.

Double check your markings against your pattern tissue before you stitch.

■ If you have pockets on both sides of the garment, make sure that they are positioned in the same place and the same direction on both sides.

Prepare welting strips according to the directions on your pattern guidesheet or refer to Welting, page 32.

Interface pocket flaps for a more professional finish.

■ Refer to Interfacing, page 86.

Check the length of the finished pocket flaps against the length of the pocket markings on your garment—they must be identical.

APPLYING WELT POCKETS

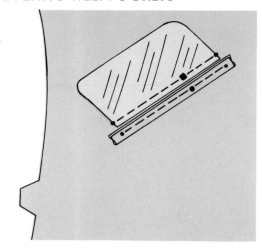

Stitch the welts and completed pocket flaps to your garment following the specific instructions included on your pattern guidesheet.

Match the pocket flaps and welts to the garment carefully when you are using fabrics such as plaids or stripes.

Backstitch to reinforce the corners of the pocket at the beginning and end of the stitching.

■ Use small stitches, about 15–20 per inch (every 25 mm), for secure, permanent pockets.

Check all stitching lines for accuracy.

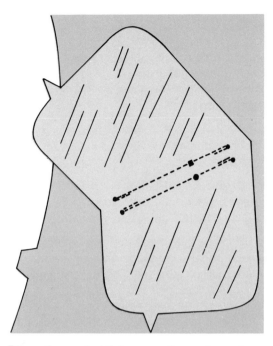

Place the pocket lining over the welts and flaps, then match the markings *very* carefully.

■ There is a definite top and bottom to most welt pockets.

Be sure that both the center markings and the corners are matched correctly.

Stitch the pocket lining to the garment.

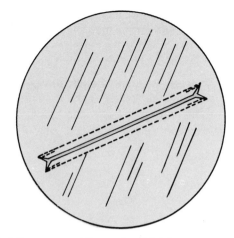

Cut the garment through all thicknesses between the stitching lines.

■ Clip a "V" into the corners all the way to, but not through, the stitching.

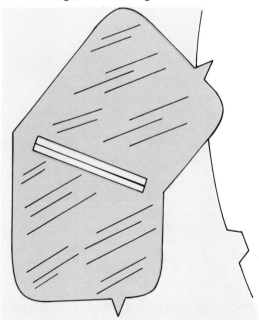

Pull the pocket lining through the opening to the wrong side of the garment and press.

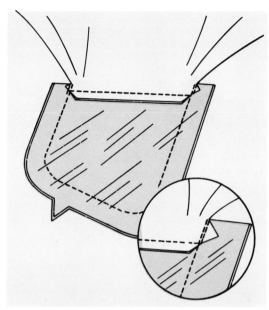

Complete the pocket by stitching around the edge of the pocket lining on the stitching line.

■ Sew through the lining and the "V" clips, keeping the garment free.

■ Use a zipper foot to sew exactly on the stitching line.

Reinforce the ends of the pocket opening with small machine stitches, about 15-20 per inch (each 25 mm), through the "V" clips.

ruffles

Ruffles are just right to add a fashion touch on a blouse, dress or formal men's shirt. They are also used for home decorating items including sheets, pillows, dust ruffles and curtains.

Follow your pattern guidesheet to make Straight or Circular Ruffles. Both types of softly gathered fabric strips allow you to trim a project easily, in style.

straight ruffles

Straight ruffles are made from a strip of fabric that is gathered and then stitched to the garment. Ruffles can be either Single- or Double-Edge.

- A Single-Edge Ruffle is finished on one edge, gathered and stitched in a seam on the other edge.

- A Double-Edge Ruffle is finished on both edges, gathered somewhere in between and stitched to the right side of the garment.

A ruffle should be made from a length of fabric at least 2½ to 3 times longer than the area where it will be attached. This will give you enough fullness for a good-looking trim. A good rule of thumb to remember is the wider the ruffle or the sheerer the fabric, the fuller the ruffle should be.

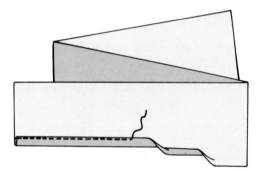

Finish the outer edge of a single-edge ruffle or both edges of a double-edge ruffle with a narrow or rolled hem.

- Refer to Hems, page 84, for more information.

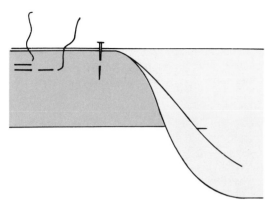

- On lightweight fabrics, such as sheers, this simple hint lets you avoid finishing the hem edge: Fold the ruffle in half lengthwise, pin the raw edges together and gather the ruffle through both thicknesses.

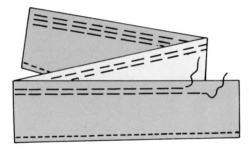

Gather the ruffle.

- See Gathering, page 72, for details about this technique.

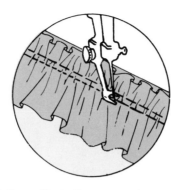

Stitch the ruffle to the garment.

- Join a single-edge ruffle to a garment with the ruffle on top to prevent stitching tucks into the seam.

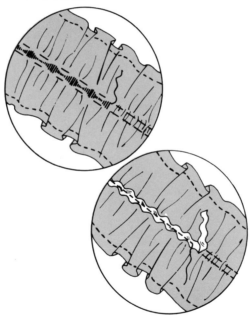

- Decorative stitches can be used to join a double-edge ruffle to the garment. Stitch between the gathering, through all thicknesses, or stitch a trim on top of the gathering stitches to cover them. Rickrack works fine.

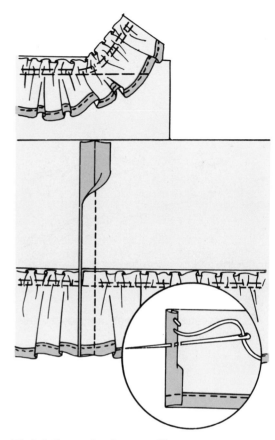

Finish the ends of your ruffle.

- You can taper the ends into the seamline, stitch them into a cross seam or turn the edge to the wrong side and slipstitch.

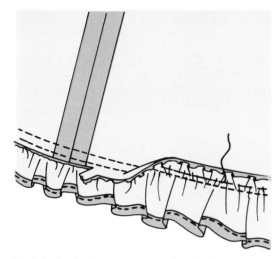

Finish the inside raw edge of a single-edge ruffle by making a second row of stitching ¼" (6 mm) from the seamline.

Trim off the seam allowances, just beyond this second stitching line.

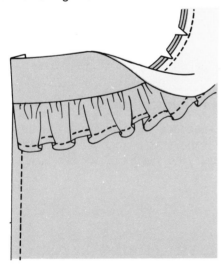

Sometimes your pattern will include a shaped facing or suggest a bias facing to finish the raw edge. Refer to Facings, page 64, for more information.

circular ruffles

Circular ruffles are cut from a circular pattern piece. The smaller circular edge is stitched to the garment edge; the larger circular edge creates the fullness to form a ruffle.

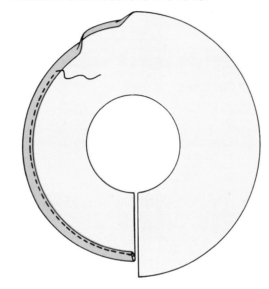

Finish the outer edge of the ruffle with a narrow or rolled hem.

■ Refer to Hems, page 84.

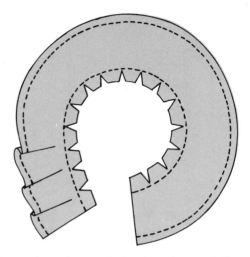

Staystitch the small circular edge and clip to, but not through, the stitches.

Stitch the small circular edge to the edge of the garment, right sides together.

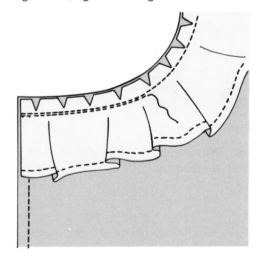

■ Keep the ruffle of your garment on top as you sew to help prevent stitching tucks into the seam.

■ Keep the raw edges even as you stitch by basting first, if necessary.

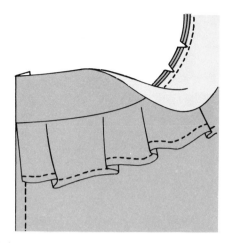

Finish the inside edge with a shaped or bias facing.

■ Refer to your pattern guidesheet or Facings, page 64, for more information.

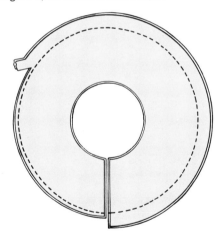

On lightweight or sheer fabrics, you can make a ruffle from two layers of fabric for an easy, elegant finish.

Cut two ruffles and stitch the outer circular edge, right sides together.

Trim and notch the seam allowances.

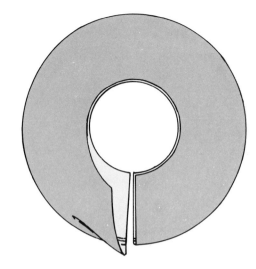

Turn the ruffle right sides out and follow the instructions on your pattern guidesheet to attach the ruffle to your garment.

113

seams

Seams are lines of stitching used to join two or more pieces of fabric together.

Most often the seams in a garment are made with straight or zigzag stitches and are called Plain Seams. There are times, however, when more detailed or decorative seams are in order. Once you learn how to construct a French Seam, a Double-Stitched Seam, a Flat-Felled Seam, a Welt Seam and a Lapped Seam, you'll have a whole range of sewing skills, useful for any project you want to try.

plain seam

This is the seam used most often to join fabric pieces in a typical garment.

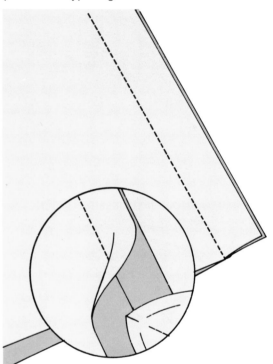

Place the two pieces of fabric right sides together, matching seamlines.

■ Be certain the cut edges of the seam allowances rest one on top of another.

Stitch along the seamline.

Press the seam flat, as it was stitched; then open the seam allowances and press again.

french seam

This enclosed seam is used on sheer or lightweight fabrics as a combination seam and seam finish. It works well on straight or moderately shaped seams. Avoid using the French seam in areas involving ease or opposite curves because it doesn't provide the flexibility you need in such situations.

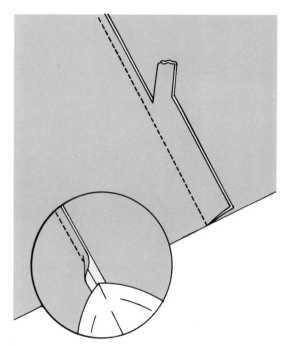

Stitch the two pieces of fabric, wrong sides together, ⅜″ (10 mm) from the raw edges.

Trim the seam allowances to ⅛″ (3 mm).

Press the seam allowances open with the tip of your iron.

■ It helps to finger press first: Open the seam allowances with the tips of your fingers and run them along the seam.

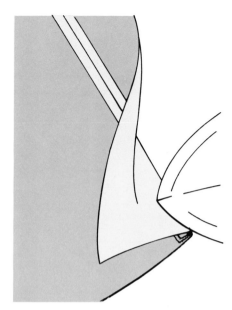

Fold the fabric over the seam allowances, right sides together, so that the seam rests at the edge of the fold; press.

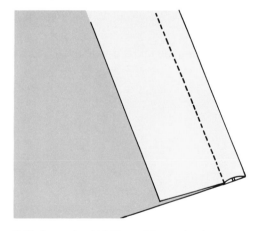

Stitch again, ¼″ (6 mm) from the folded edge.

■ The two seams, ⅜″ (10 mm) and ¼″ (6 mm), combine to make a ⅝″ (15 mm) seam.

double-stitched seam

The double-stitched seam is used in the same manner as the French seam but is also useful on curves or in other areas where a French seam would be difficult to make. A double-stitched seam is often used on knit fabrics.

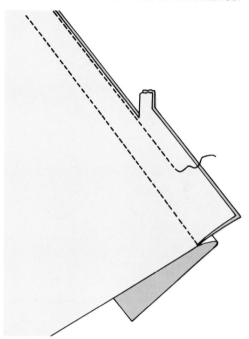

Stitch on the seamline, right sides of the two pieces of fabric together.

Stitch again, about ⅜″ (10 mm) from the seam, closer to the cut edges of the seam allowances.

Trim the seam allowances close to the stitching.

115

flat-felled seam

This enclosed seam is decorative as well as durable. Often used on sportswear, it looks like a welt seam on one side and a lapped seam on the other.

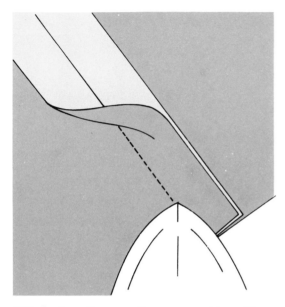

Stitch along the seamline, wrong sides of the two pieces of fabric together.

Press the seam allowances open, then press them to one side.

■ Be sure you press all similar seams in the same direction.

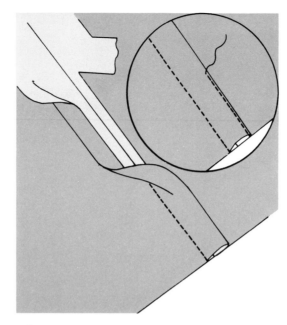

Trim the under seam allowance to ⅛″ (3 mm).

Fold the edge of the upper seam allowance under ¼″ (6 mm) and press over the trimmed seam allowance.

Edgestitch along the fold, through all thicknesses.

mock flat-felled seam

This modified version, used in the same places as the flat-felled seam, has the advantage of being easier to handle at corners and curves. However, it does not provide a finished appearance on the wrong side.

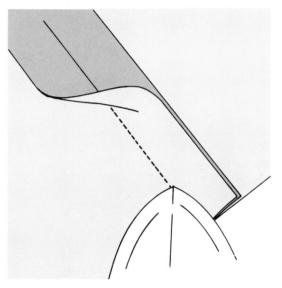

Stitch along the seamline, right sides of the two pieces of fabric together.

Press the seam allowances open, then press them to one side.

■ Be sure you press all similar seams in the same direction.

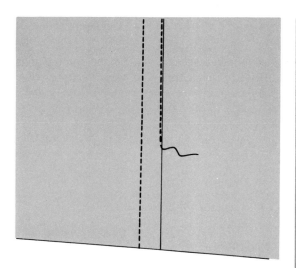

Topstitch on the right side ¼″ (6 mm) from the seam, through the garment and the seam allowances.

Edgestitch on the right side along the seamline, through the garment and the seam allowances.

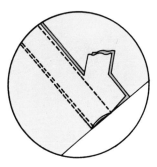

Trim the seam allowances close to the stitching if necessary to eliminate bulk.

welt seam

This is a topstitched seam used as a decorative finish. It also holds seam allowances in place on the wrong side of the garment and acts as a seam finish to prevent fabric from fraying.

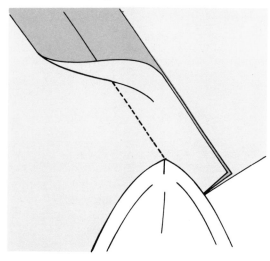

Stitch along the seamline, right sides of the two pieces of fabric together.

Press the seam allowances open, then press to one side.

- Be sure to press all similar seams in the same direction.

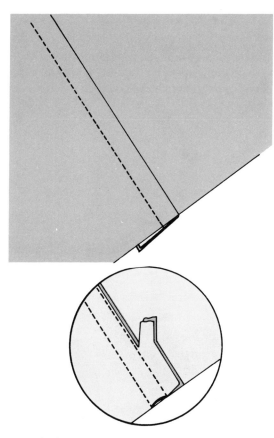

Topstitch on the right side ¼″ (6 mm) from the seam, through the garment and the seam allowances.

Trim the seam allowances close to the stitching if necessary to eliminate bulk.

lapped seam

The lapped seam is used, as a rule, for natural or synthetic leather and suede. It has the appearance of the flat-felled seam.

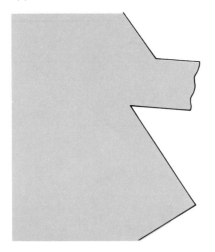

Trim away the full width of one seam allowance.

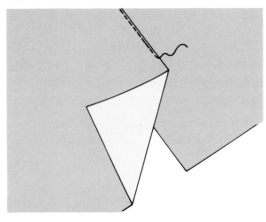

Place the wrong side of the trimmed edge along the seamline of the other section on the right side.

Edgestitch along the trimmed edge.

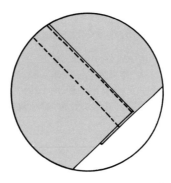

Topstitch ¼″ (6 mm) from the stitching and through both thicknesses.

seams which join opposite corners

Sometimes you'll need to join an inward corner to an outward corner or a straight edge because of special design features such as lapels, gussets or details on certain types of collars or sleeves.

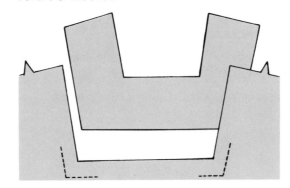

Reinforce the inward corner with small stitches (about 20 per inch or stitches approximately 1.5 mm long).

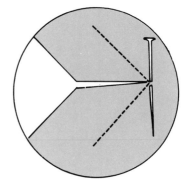

Clip to, but not through, the stitches.

- Place a pin at the corner to prevent clipping too far.

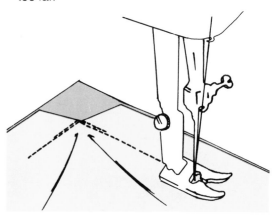

Follow the directions on the pattern guidesheet to position the two corners correctly for sewing.

Match the seamlines along one edge, with the clipped side up.

Stitch to the clipped corner.

- Leave the needle in the fabric.

Raise the presser foot and pivot the fabric.

Lower the presser foot and continue stitching.

curved seams

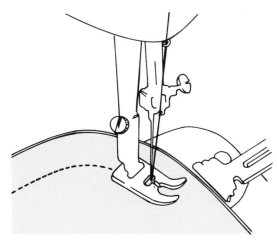

Stitching around a curved area is not difficult. Just remember to keep your eye on the edge of the fabric as you line it up with the seamline marking or seam gauge attachment on your machine. Stitch slowly and carefully so the finished curve will be smooth.

seams which join opposite curves

Occasionally you'll be joining two differently shaped curves, such as on a raglan sleeve or princess seamline. With a minimum amount of skill and a bit of confidence you can stitch them perfectly by matching the raw edges and guiding the fabric carefully as you sew. If you need some help keeping the edges even on extreme curves, follow these steps.

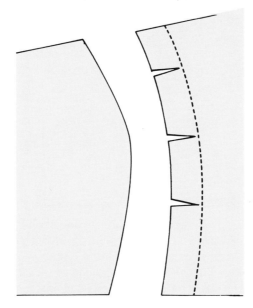

Reinforce the inside curve with small machine stitches, approximately 20 per inch (each 25 mm).

Clip the seam allowance at several places to release it and allow it to spread to meet the outside curve.

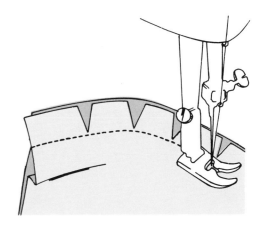

Match the seamlines and stitch with the clipped side on top.

Control the fullness of the fabric with your fingers so that both layers of fabric move through the machine evenly.

removing stitches

Mistakes do happen, so you must know how to remove stitches from a seam without stretching the fabric or causing snags.

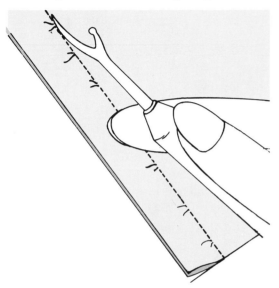

Use a seam ripper or small scissors and cut the threads on one side every 2″ (50 mm) or so. Pull the thread on the opposite side and remove the short threads from the clipped side.

trimming and grading seam allowances

Trimming and grading are methods of cutting away some of the seam allowance to reduce bulk.

- Generally, when trimming is necessary, about half of the seam allowance is cut away. Exact amounts are suggested for things such as a French seam where a specific amount must be trimmed to complete the technique.

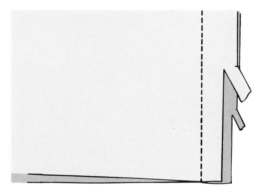

- Grading means simply cutting the seam allowances to different widths to layer them. It is done on enclosed seams to prevent a ridge from showing along the trimmed edge. The seam allowance which rests next to the outside of the garment should be the widest.

clipping and notching seam allowances

Clipping and notching are methods of slitting the seam allowances in corners or along curves to allow them to lie smooth.

- Clipping is done by cutting into the seam allowance with the point of your scissors. Never clip an area before you sew it, either with a seamline or reinforcing stitches. It's important that you clip all the way to, but not through, the stitches.

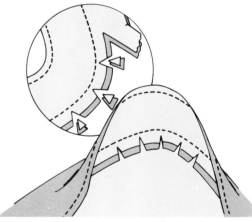

- Notching is done by cutting tiny wedges from the seam allowance. It helps remove excess bulk from outward curves that are pressed to form an inward curve, such as at the edge of a patch pocket or collar. Notching is necessary only when the overlap of the clips causes excess bulk. It tends to weaken the seam allowance, so notch with caution.

seam finishes

Often seam finishes are used to give the inside of a garment a professional look. Seam finishes are necessary only when the fabric ravels or frays.

The seam-finishing technique you choose will depend on your fabric and whether it ravels as well as whether the seams will be seen when the garment is worn.

Seam finishes are done *after* the seams of the garment are stitched—not a moment before.

pinked finish

This quick and easy finish works well on firmly woven fabrics.

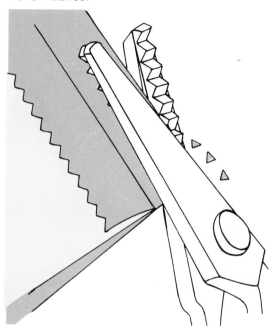

Press the seam open.

Pink the cut edges of the seam allowances with pinking shears.

■ You should only trim away small triangles of fabric. Do not cut into the seam allowances.

turned and stitched finish

For a clean edge that is attractive and functional, use this finish. It is suitable for light to medium weight fabrics, and is especially attractive in unlined jackets.

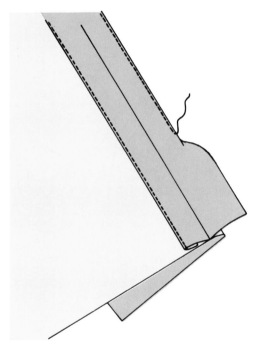

Press the seam open.

Fold seam allowances under ¼″ (6 mm) from the edge and press.

Edgestitch along the fold.

overcast finish

This hand finish works well on most fabrics. It is especially good for sheer fabrics such as organdy or chiffon.

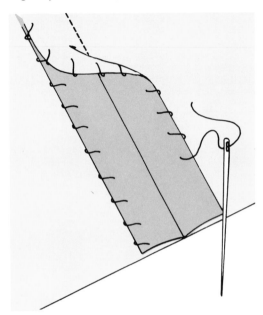

Press the seam open.

Make overcast stitches over the edge of the seam allowance evenly spaced and at a uniform depth.

- For additional information on the overcast stitch, refer to Hand Sewing, page 80.

machine zigzag finish

The zigzag finish is one of the most useful seam finishes for fabrics that fray. It is also good for seam allowances which are finished together in curved areas such as armholes and crotches.

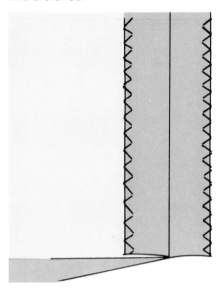

Press the seam open.

Stitch over the edge with a zigzag stitch set at a medium width—12-15 stitches per inch (every 25 mm).

If you're working with seam allowances which are finished together, follow these steps.

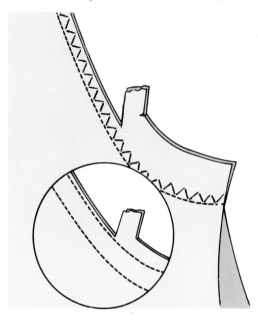

1. Press the seam allowances together.

2. Make a zigzag machine stitch close to the seamline, through all thicknesses. If you do not have a zigzag stitch on your machine, make a second row of stitches about ¼" (6 mm) from the seam into the seam allowance.

3. Trim seam allowances close to the stitches.

the hong kong finish

This finish is suitable for medium to heavy fabrics. It is especially attractive on unlined coats and jackets.

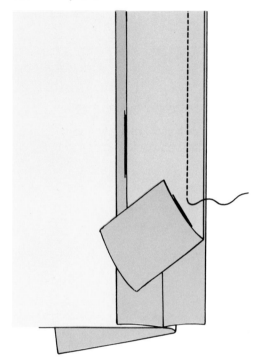

Press the seam open.

Cut bias strips, about 1" (25 mm) wide, from a lightweight fabric.

Place the bias strip and the seam allowance right sides together, and stitch ¼" (6 mm) from the raw edge.

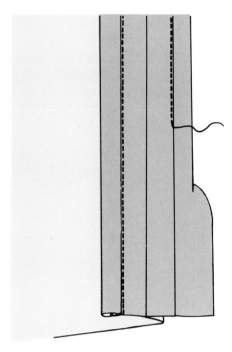

Flip the bias strip over the raw edge to the underside, and stitch in the ridge of the first stitching line.

- The "stitch-in-the-ditch" method works well. Refer to Machine Sewing, page 96.

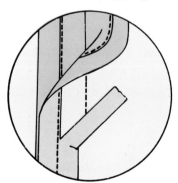

Trim the bias close to the stitches.

bound finish

The bound finish is used for seams in medium to heavyweight fabrics such as heavy corduroy, fleece or fake fur.

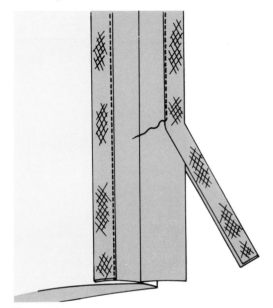

Press the seam open.

Slip double-fold bias tape over the raw edge of the seam allowance, with the wider edge of the tape on the underside of the seam allowance.

Edgestitch along the fold from the topside.

If your seams are finished together, as in the armhole of an unlined jacket, follow these steps.

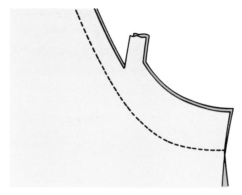

1. Press the seam allowances together.

2. Trim the seam allowances to about ¼″ (6 mm) from the seam and clip or notch, as necessary.

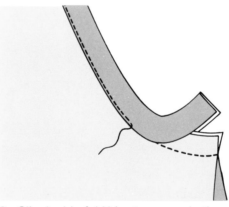

3. Slip double-fold bias tape over both seam allowances, with the wider edge of the tape on the underside.

4. Edgestitch along the fold of the bias tape through all thicknesses.

self-bound finish

This is used on light to medium weight fabrics such as percale, gingham or chambray. It is a combination seam and seam finish.

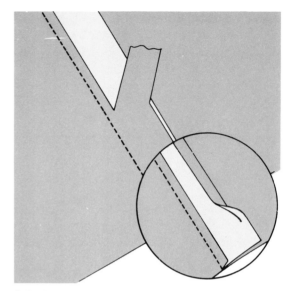

Stitch a plain seam.

Trim one seam allowance to ⅛″ (3 mm).

Turn under the edge of the other seam allowance ⅛″ (3 mm) and press.

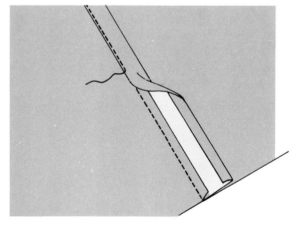

Turn the folded edge over the trimmed seam allowance, matching it to the seam.

Edgestitch close to the fold, on the seam allowance, through all thicknesses.

sleeves

There's no need to be up in arms about sewing sleeves. They're not difficult, if you follow the suggestions in this section.

Sleeves generally are divided into four basic types: Set-In Sleeves, Shirt Sleeves, Raglan Sleeves and Kimono Sleeves. Each type requires some special techniques which are easy enough to master.

set-in sleeve

This is a shaped sleeve that is eased or gathered into the armhole of the garment over the shoulder. It is used in all types of garments. You can learn to attach a set-in sleeve perfectly in no time at all, with two rows of easestitching or a single row of ease-plus stitching.

EASESTITCHING A SLEEVE CAP

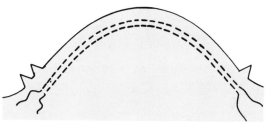

Stitch two rows of easestitching, about 8-10 stitches per inch (every 25 mm), around the top of the sleeve cap, from notch to notch.

- The first row of stitching should be on the seamline and the second ¼″ (6 mm) away, toward the cut edge of the seam allowance.

125

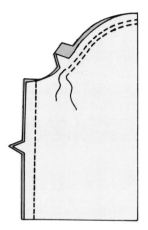

Stitch the underarm sleeve seam.

■ Some jacket and coat sleeves will have two seams.

Pull the bobbin thread ends to ease the fullness evenly along the sleeve cap.

EASE-PLUS METHOD FOR A SLEEVE CAP

In the Ease-Plus Method, you only use a single row of stitching to gather up the fullness in a sleeve cap. This technique is very easy and some sewing experts think it works best. By all means, try it.

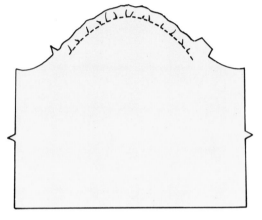

Place the curved edge of the sleeve on the machine so that you will be stitching right on the seamline.

Stitch, starting at one side edge, using a regular size straight stitch.

Begin ease-plus stitching at the first notch by placing one forefinger on each side of the presser foot and pushing the fabric backward so that it passes under the needle faster than it would move ordinarily.

■ As you become more experienced with this technique, you'll know how fast to push the fabric through the machine. However, if at first you gather too much ease and the sleeve cap is too small, just clip stitches every 2″ (50 mm) or so. If you need to pull in more ease to make the sleeve cap smaller, use a pin or crochet hook to pull up stitches at regular intervals.

Stitch the underarm seam to finish the sleeve piece.

SEWING THE SLEEVE IN PLACE

No matter what method you used to gather the fullness of the sleeve cap, follow these steps to sew the sleeve in place.

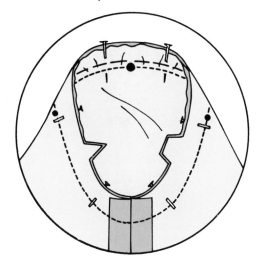

Turn garment inside out.

Hold the garment so that you are looking inside the sleeve.

Place the sleeve in position under the garment with right sides together.

Match the seamlines and notches of the garment and the sleeve exactly.

Roll the garment and sleeve over your forefinger to distribute the extra fullness as you pin the sleeve into the armhole.

Place the pins so the heads are resting near the cut edge.

- This will help you remove them easily when you are sewing.

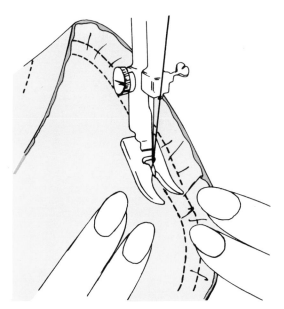

Stitch the sleeve cap to the armhole with the sleeve side up, controlling the fullness of the fabric with your fingers to prevent tucks and puckers.

- It's a good idea to use a narrow zigzag stitch to sew the sleeve in place because it helps to ease in the fabric and gives more stretch to the armhole seam.

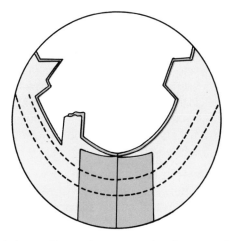

Reinforce the underarm section from notch to notch with a second row of stitches about ¼″ (6 mm) into the seam allowance.

Trim the underarm seam allowances between the notches.

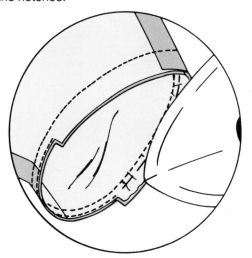

Press the seam allowances together from the inside of the garment.

- The seam allowances should face inside the sleeve when the garment is worn.

127

shirt sleeve

The shirt sleeve is a type of set-in sleeve with a shallower sleeve cap curve. Because of this, it has less fullness than a regular set-in sleeve. It is attached to the body of the garment before the side seams are sewn. That way, you can sew on a flat piece to get a smoother sleeve cap on the finished garment.

The shirt sleeve is used on men's or women's tailored shirts and sports shirts as well as on fashion shirts with dropped shoulders.

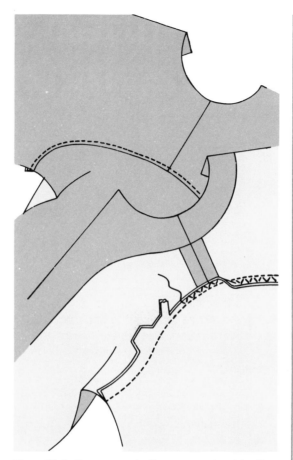

Topstitch the seams to the garment or trim the seam allowances close to the stitching and finish with a zigzag stitch.

- If you don't have a zigzag stitch on your machine, just make a second row of stitches ¼″ (6 mm) from the first row through both seam allowances.

- Trim the seam allowances close to the stitching.

- Press seam allowances toward the sleeve.

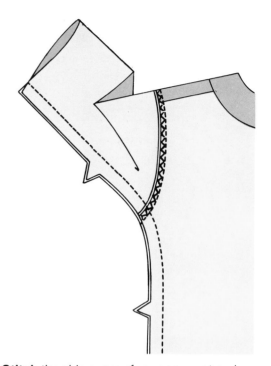

Stitch the side seam of your garment and sleeve.

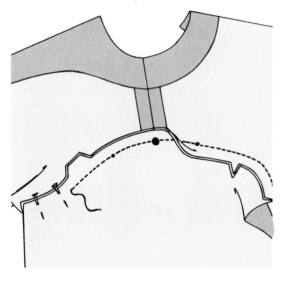

Pin the sleeve into the armhole, right sides together, matching the markings.

- Leave the underarm sleeve seam and side seam open.

Stitch, with the sleeve side up, easing any fullness with your fingers as you sew.

Press the seam allowances away from the sleeve, toward the garment.

raglan sleeve

The raglan sleeve is attached to the garment in the front and back by diagonal seams running from the neckline to the underarm. It adds design interest to a garment and is comfortable to wear.

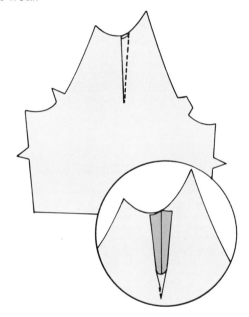

Stitch the dart at the shoulder.

- See Darts, page 62.

- Some raglan sleeves will have a seam instead of a dart.

Press the dart or seam open.

- For a smooth, even curve, press over a tailor's ham or press mitt.

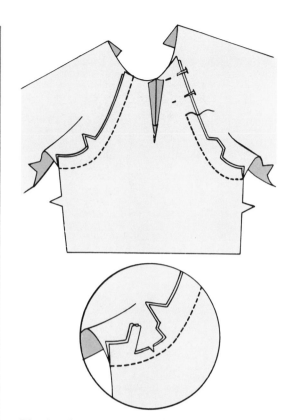

Pin the diagonal seams of the sleeve to your garment, right sides together, matching the markings.

Stitch along the seamline, keeping the raw edges even.

Trim and clip the seam allowances close to the stitches between the notches at the underarm.

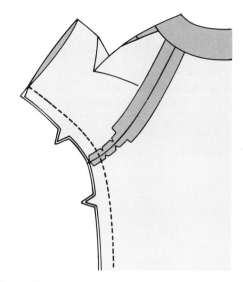

Press the seam open.

Stitch the side seam of the garment and the sleeve seam.

129

kimono sleeve

The kimono sleeve is nothing more than a seam! It is cut as part of your garment with a shoulder and underarm seam. If the sleeve is designed to fit close to the body, it probably will have a gusset, which is a small fabric insert, under the arm. Your pattern guidesheet will include detailed instructions for making a gusset correctly. To sew the kimono sleeve itself, follow these steps.

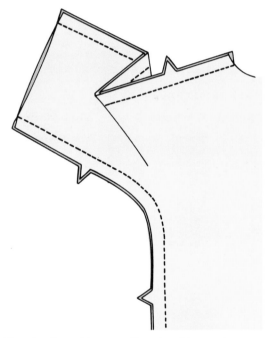

Match all markings on the shoulder and underarm seams as you pin baste them.

Sew seams with a regular stitch.

Reinforce the underarm by using small stitches, about 15-20 per inch (every 25 mm), along the underarm curve.

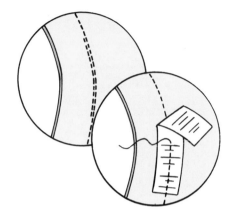

■ Either make a second line of stitches or sew a piece of seam tape to the seamline at the underarm area to give it extra strength.

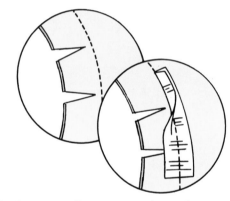

Clip the seam allowances at the underarm curve to, but not through, the stitches.

■ Be careful not to clip into the tape.

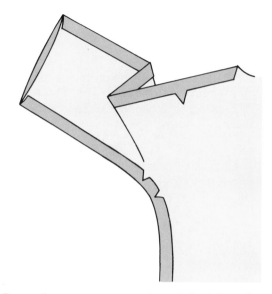

Press the seams open using a tailor's ham for the curved area.

sleeve openings

There's more than one way to open and close a buttoned cuff. In fact, a sleeve can have a Dart Opening, Continuous Lap Opening, Faced Opening or a Placket Opening.

Your pattern guidesheet will always give you complete directions for making a sleeve opening suited to your garment. Of course, you may want to be a bit creative and try a new technique.

You'll find details about the Placket Opening in the section on Bands, page 20. For some suggestions about making the other types of sleeve openings, read on.

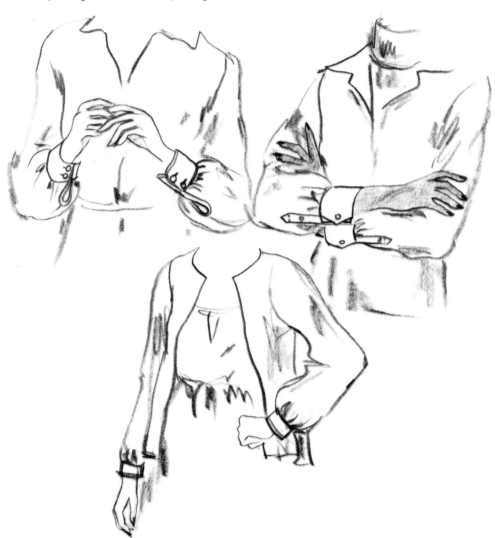

dart opening

This is a quick and easy method used on many fashions.

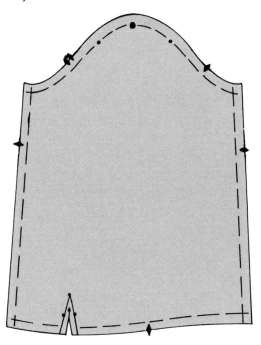

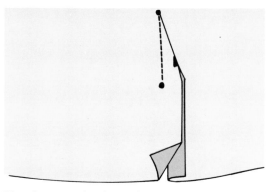

The dart opening is made by sewing a small dart which ends with the wide part about 2" (50 mm) above the edge of the sleeve.

Stitch from the wide end of the dart to the point, following your pattern markings.

Slash the dart to form an opening as the pattern indicates.

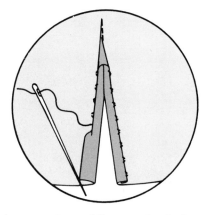

Roll the raw edges of the opening to the wrong side of the garment and slipstitch.

continuous lap opening

This method binds the raw edges of the opening with a separate strip of fabric.

Cut a piece of fabric for the binding 1¼" (32 mm) wide and twice the length of the slash marking.

- Use either the True Bias or the straight grain of the fabric.

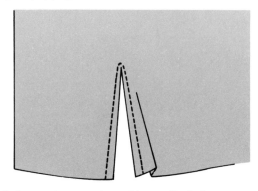

Reinforce the opening with small stitches, about 20 per inch (every 25 mm) along the stitching line as marked on your pattern tissue.

- Or, stitch a narrow "V" long enough for the opening, usually about 3" (75 mm).

Slash the fabric between the reinforcement stitching, cutting up to, but not through, the stitches.

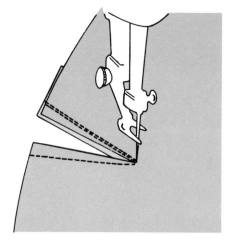

Stitch the right side of the binding to the wrong side of the sleeve along the reinforcement stitches to the point of the slash.

Leave the needle in the fabric and raise the presser foot.

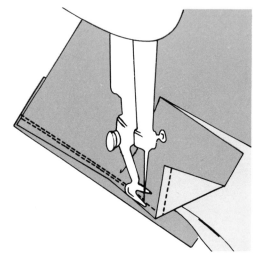

Spread the slash and place the binding along the lower edge.

Lower the presser foot and continue stitching.

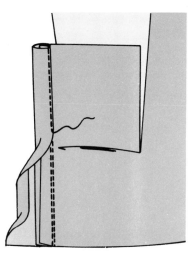

Flip the binding over the raw edge.

Turn the raw edge of the binding under, then place the folded edge along the seamline.

Edgestitch through all thicknesses of fabric from the right side of the garment.

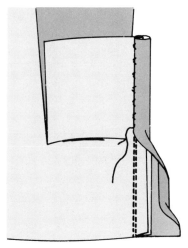

■ To finish the binding by hand, follow the same steps but machine stitch the binding and garment right sides together, then slipstitch from the wrong side.

faced opening

A faced opening is extra fast, and easy too. It's used on many types of sleeves.

Cut a small reinforcement patch from tightly woven lightweight fabric.

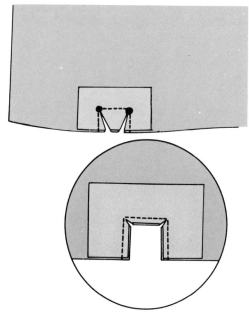

Place the patch on the sleeve edge, right sides together, over the placement markings.

Stitch the patch to the seam allowance following the markings.

Clip the seam allowances and the patch to the corners, but not through the stitching.

Trim the remaining seam allowances.

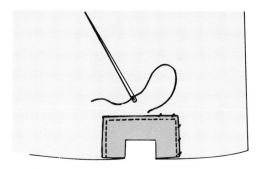

Flip the patch to the wrong side and press.

Finish the edges of the patch and whipstitch it to the sleeve.

trims

Add your own touch of beauty to the garments you make with fashion trims.

Rickrack, braid, ribbon and appliqués are available in any color, size and shape. Choose the trim which suits you best.

Then apply it following the simple steps for the Flat Method, the Edging Method or the Inserted Method of putting trims right where they look fine.

flat method

This method can be used for any trim that is finished on both edges. Rickrack, appliqués, soutache and braids all fall into this category.

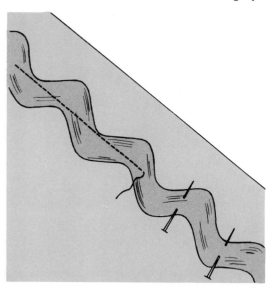

Baste the trim in place along the placement line, either with pins or long basting stitches.

Stitch the trim to the garment.

- Extra wide trim requires stitching along both edges.

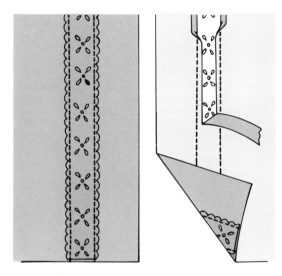

Apply a lacy or openwork trim for a see-through effect. Stitch both edges to the garment, then trim away the fabric which rests underneath the trim.

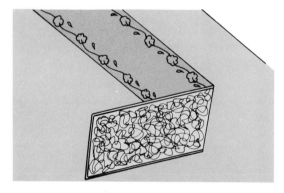

Flat trims for straight or slightly curved areas—such as along the bottom of a skirt, jacket, vest or wide sleeve—can be attached with fusible web. Refer to Fusing, page 17. Test a sample of your fabric and trim first to be sure they will withstand the heat and steam required for fusing. Keep in mind that fusing is not useful for areas which are sharply curved or have many corners.

CORNERS AND CURVES

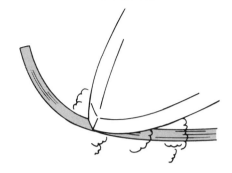

Shape the trim around curves by pressing it with a steam iron before applying it to the garment.

■ A flexible or narrow trim works best on curves.

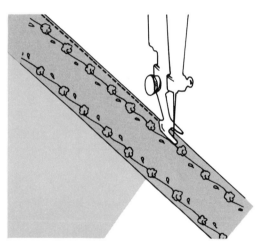

Miter the corners of wide trims by first stitching the trim in place to the corner along the outside edge of the trim.

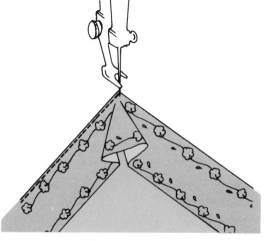

Lift the presser foot of your machine and, with the needle in place, turn the trim and the fabric in the other direction.

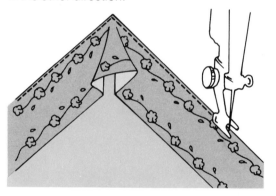

Lower the presser foot and continue stitching.

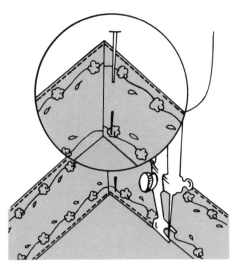

Fold a neat miter, a diagonal fold, in the trim at the corner and pin in place.

Stitch the inside edge of the trim.

Stitch the mitered fold.

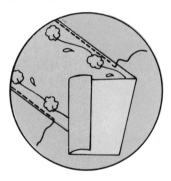

Finish the trim ends by neatly turning them under before stitching them to the garment.

edging method

This application is used for trims with one finished edge, such as pregathered lace, eyelet, piping and fringe. The trim can be applied to the edge of the garment or caught in a seam.

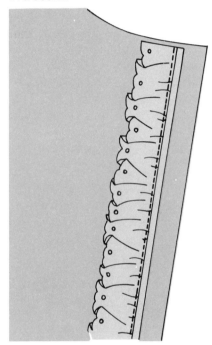

Stitch the trim to the garment along the edge or seamline, right sides together, with the trim toward the garment.

- Use a zipper foot attachment on your machine to allow you to stitch close to the trim.

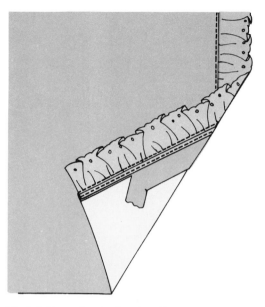

Finish the edge by turning the seam allowance to the inside and topstitching through all thicknesses.

- Or edgestitch through the trim and seam allowance, then cut off the excess seam allowance.

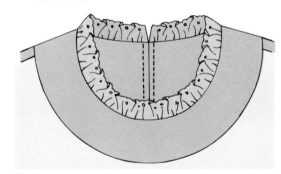

Some patterns include a shaped or bias facing as an inside finish. Refer to Facings, page 64.

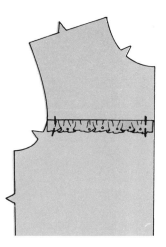

If your edging trim is to be sewn in a seam, pin baste the trim along one seam allowance. Next place the other section of fabric on top of it. Sew along the seamline to complete the seam and attach the trim in the same step.

CORNERS AND CURVES

Ease the trim gently around corners or curved areas by using your fingers to pull it slightly as it passes under the sewing machine needle.

Keep the trim properly positioned over the stitching line.

Turn corners smoothly by first stitching the trim to the corner.

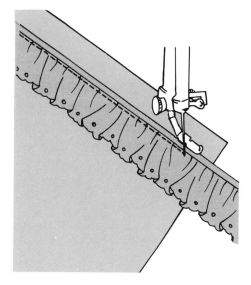

Leave the needle in position in the fabric.

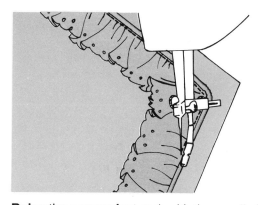

Raise the presser foot and, with the needle in place, turn the trim to pivot it and the fabric around the corner.

Lower the presser foot and continue stitching.

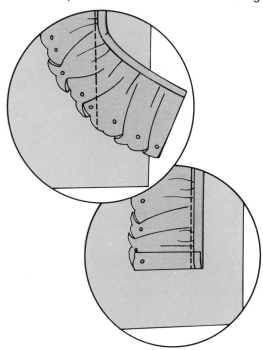

Finish the ends by tapering the trim into the seam allowance or by turning them under and hemming them with hand or machine stitching.

inserted method

This application can be used with many types of trim, including those with two unfinished edges.

The method works best for straight sections, such as the front of a blouse or the bottom of a jacket or skirt. It is not suitable for corners or curves.

Follow the instructions on your pattern guidesheet or add the trim to an area you want to highlight by following these steps.

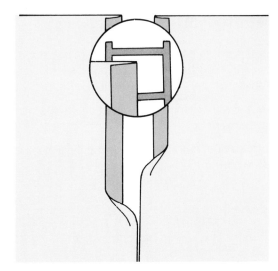

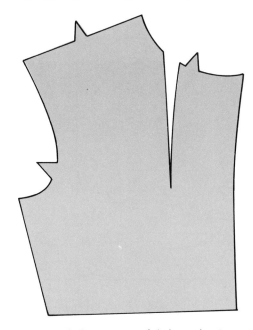

Mark a slash line on your fabric and cut the fabric.

Press the edges along the slash to the wrong side of the fabric.

- The width of each turned-back edge should be half the width of the exposed area of the trim.

Place the folded edges of the slash along the trim and edgestitch through all thicknesses.

tucks

A tuck is a narrow fold of fabric stitched in place to add design interest, control fullness or help shape a garment.

Tucks are used often near the shoulder, yoke or waistline area. Sometimes they are used strictly for a fashion touch on collars or cuffs.

Tucks can be stitched to rest on the outside or inside of the garment. Follow your pattern guidesheet for exact stitching directions.

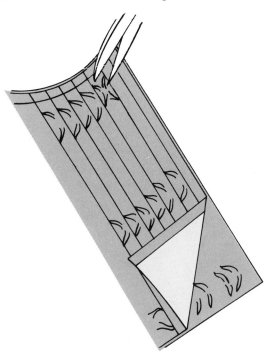

Mark each tuck with a method suitable for the fabric.

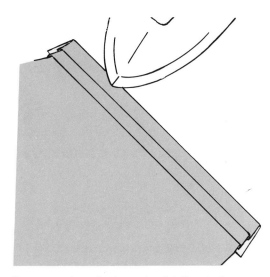

Press each tuck along the foldline before you stitch.

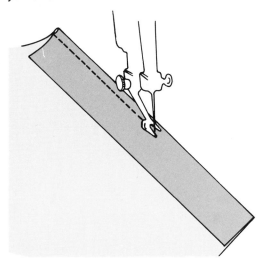

Stitch the tucks along the stitching line.

Use the foldline of the tuck as a guide for stitching, following these steps.

1. Determine the width of the tuck from the markings on your pattern tissue.

2. Place the fold of the tuck next to the presser foot or one of the needle plate markings.

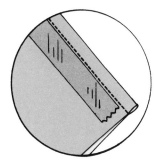

■ Special sewing tape available at a notions store can be finger pressed lightly on the fabric to serve as a stitching guide. See Machine Stitching, page 97.

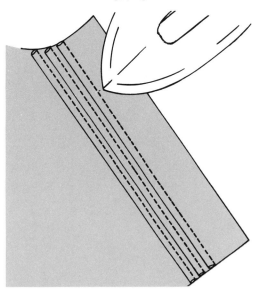

Press each tuck flat as it was stitched, then press them all in the direction indicated on the pattern guidesheet.

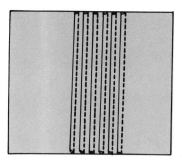

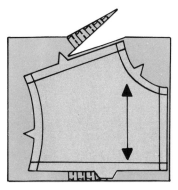

Many of today's fashions include tucks. Save yourself some work but don't sacrifice good looks—fold and stitch tucks in position before you place the pattern piece on the fabric.

Then, pin the piece where it belongs and cut it out. You'll have tucks in no time for pockets, yokes or other areas.

waistline finishes

Just like other edges of a garment, the waistline must be finished so that it will lie smoothly and fit comfortably.

Your pattern guidesheet will recommend a specific waistline finish. Most often it will be one of these three methods: Waistband, Facing or Casing.

Follow these general waistline finishing facts as you work.

waistbands

A waistband is a narrow strip of fabric sewn onto the waistline of the garment. As a rule, a waistband should be a bit snug but still have about 1″ (25 mm) ease to keep the waistband from feeling too tight.

There are two types of waistbands, Straight and Contoured.

- A Straight Waistband is made from a straight strip of fabric. It rests above the natural waistline when the garment is worn.

- A Contoured Waistband is cut from a shaped strip of fabric. It curves to fit the natural shape of the body when the garment is worn.

Both types of waistbands are attached to the garment in the same way, although the straight waistband usually has a fold along the upper edge while the top edge of the contoured waistband has a seam.

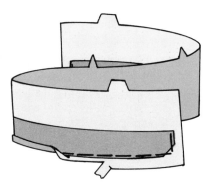

Interface the waistband as your pattern guidesheet suggests.

- See further instructions on Interfacing, page 86.

Turn the unnotched long side of the waistband toward the wrong side of the fabric and press it in position along the seamline.

- Baste close to the folded edge if necessary.

Trim the seam allowance to ¼″ (6 mm) from the seamline.

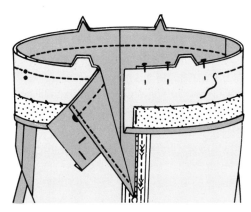

Place the right side of the untrimmed waistband edge on the wrong side of the garment, matching notches or other markings, and pin baste.

- Always be sure that this seam is accurate before you sew. To check, flip the pin-basted waistband piece up and over the raw edge of the garment. Does it cover the raw edge so that the right side of the band will be on the outside of the finished garment? Good. That's just as it should be.

Stitch the waistband to the garment along the seamline.

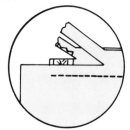

Grade the seam allowances so that the longest one rests next to the waistband itself.

Clip the seam allowances, if necessary, to relieve puckers or strain.

- This is often required on contoured waistbands.

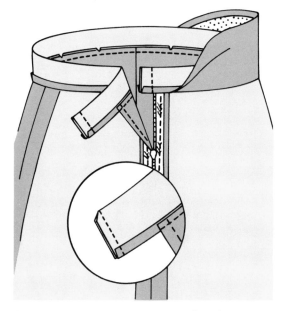

Press the seam allowances so they face upward and will rest inside the finished waistband.

Fold the ends of the waistband, right sides together, so that the long edge—trimmed and pressed, but not yet sewn—rests exactly on the seamline of the garment.

Stitch the ends of the waistband along the seamlines.

Trim the corners to remove bulk.

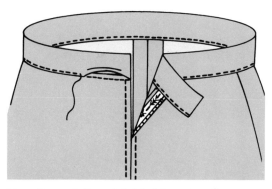

Turn the waistband right side out so it covers the seam allowances and is folded accurately across the entire length.

Press.

Edgestitch the waistband from the right side to secure it to the garment.

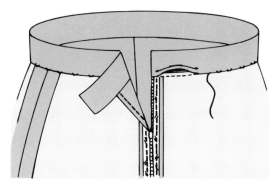

If you prefer, you can attach the waistband so that there is no edgestitching on the outside. Follow the same basic steps described above *except* start by sewing the waistband to the garment with the *right* sides of the fabric together. Next finish the side edges. Then flip the waistband up and over the seam allowances to the wrong side of the garment. Attach it using a slipstitch on the inside.

Here are a few clever ideas to eliminate bulk on a straight waistband.

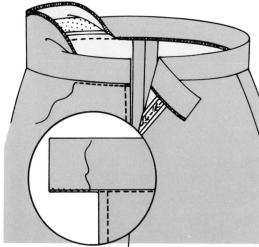

1. Place one long seamline on the selvage edge of the fabric as you cut the waistband piece.

2. Stitch the waistband to the garment, right sides together.

3. Flip the waistband over to cover the raw edge and the seam allowances so that the selvage extends just about ⅛″ (3 mm) beyond the seamline on the inside of the garment. Press.

4. "Stitch-in-the-ditch" from the right side of the garment, right below the enclosed seamline. This attaches the waistband to the wrong side of the garment.

■ See page 96, Machine Stitching, for more information on this technique.

5. Fold the seam allowances of the ends and the waistband extension under so they are enclosed in the waistband. Press.

6. Whipstitch the waistband ends and extension.

facings

A facing can be used instead of a separate waistband. This allows the finished edge of the garment to rest right at the natural waistline.

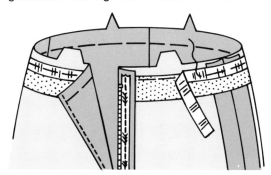

Interface the waistline edge of the garment following the directions on your pattern guidesheet.

■ Prepare the waistline seam to prevent it from stretching as the garment is worn by stitching a piece of seam tape to the inside of the garment, right on top of the seamline. Refer to the information on seam tape, page 83, for details about preshrinking and attaching it.

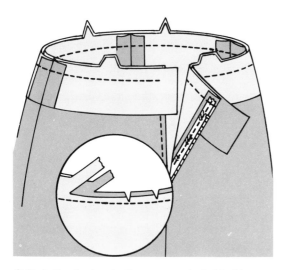

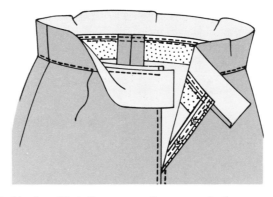

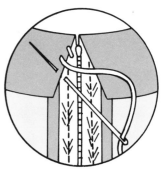

Stitch the facing to the garment, right sides together.

■ Choose a lightweight fabric for your facing when using a heavy fabric for your garment. This reduces bulk as much as possible around the waistline area.

Grade and clip the seam allowances of the waistline seam so that the longest one rests next to the outer layer of the fabric.

Press the seam allowances to rest downward, in the direction of the facing.

Understitch the seam allowances to the facing by sewing a row of stitches on the facing, just beyond the enclosed seamline.

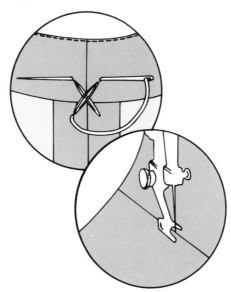

Tack the facing to the garment at the points where seams cross.

■ Use a small cross stitch done by hand or the "stitch-in-the-ditch" method by machine.

Turn under the ends of the facing to enclose them.

Whipstitch in place.

elastic casing

Elastic, of course, stretches and therefore is very convenient to use as a waistline finish. Generally the elastic is placed inside a casing. See the section on Casings, page 53, for more information. Or, follow these easy steps.

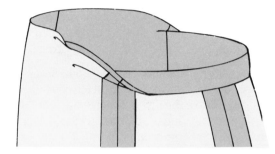

Turn the raw edge of the waistline area under ¼″ (6 mm) and press.

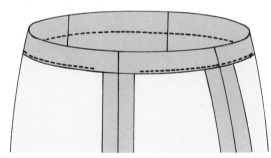

Press again along the foldline marked on the pattern piece.

- Pin baste, if necessary.

Edgestitch along the first fold you made to form a casing.

Leave a space about 1-2″ (25-50 mm) between the beginning and end of the edgestitching to make an opening in the casing to insert the elastic.

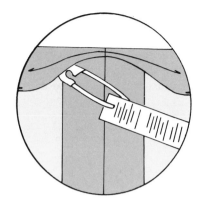

Insert the elastic, cut to the length recommended on your pattern guidesheet, using either a large safety pin or a bodkin.

- No-roll elastic and pajama elastic both work well in a waistband casing because they don't roll over or bunch up. This makes them comfortable to wear.

Overlap the cut ends of the elastic about 1″ (25 mm) or follow your pattern directions.

Stitch the ends of the elastic together.

- Use a machine zigzag stitch, if possible, because it holds the elastic best.

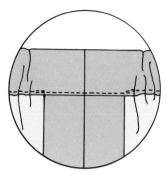

Slipstitch the opening of the casing to secure it.

- Be sure that the elastic stays where it belongs inside the casing by attaching it to the seams which cross over the casing from top to bottom. First, adjust the fabric to provide the amount of fullness you want in each section of the waistline. Then pin baste the elastic in place and "stitch-in-the-ditch." For details on this technique, see page 96.

- If you prefer to have a drawstring casing rather than elastic, see Casings, page 52.

zippers

Zippers help you slip in and out of fashion.

They were invented in 1923 by B. F. Goodrich and although there have been many improvements in zippers since then, their basic purpose remains the same. Zippers are attractive devices for fastening two sections of fabric together.

They are available in three styles: Conventional Zippers, with a closed bottom; Separating Zippers, which have an open bottom so the two sides can come apart; and Invisible Zippers, stitched to a garment in such a way that when the zipper is closed, it looks like an ordinary seam.

Zippers can be attached to a garment in a variety of ways. The methods are known as "applications" and include Centered, Lapped, Fly Front, Invisible and Exposed Applications.

Your pattern guidesheet will describe the zipper application which is best for your project. Follow the instructions to the letter and you'll find that zipper applications are easier than you might have thought.

Here are some general hints to guarantee good-looking zippers.

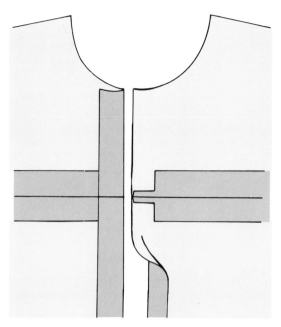

1. Eliminate as much bulk as possible before you begin applying a zipper. Where seams will cross the zipper, trim the seam allowances that will not rest directly next to the zipper to about ¼" (6 mm).

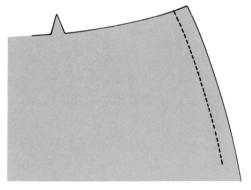

2. Staystitch any curved or bias areas along the seamlines to prevent stretching as you apply the zipper.

3. Position the zipper accurately according to the design of the garment and the type of zipper application. As a general rule, if a button, hook and eye, snap or other type of closure device will be sewn above the zipper, the zipper teeth should be about ¼" (6 mm) below the seamline at the top edge of the finished zipper. If there will not be a closure device above the zipper, the zipper teeth should rest just on the top edge of the garment, or about ⅛" (3 mm) down from it.

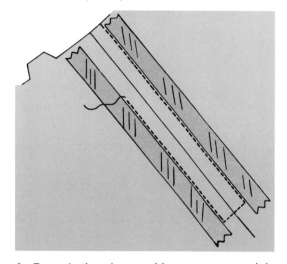

4. Baste by hand or machine or use a special self-adhesive basting tape to position the zipper accurately before you sew. Self-adhesive basting tape is available in notions departments.

5. Use the zipper foot attachment on your sewing machine as you sew a zipper in place. This attachment is designed to allow you to stitch close to the zipper for the best results.

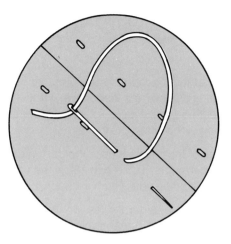

6. If you prefer, sew the zipper in place by hand rather than machine. Use a prickstitch. Refer to Hand Sewing, page 80.

centered zipper application

In this method, used for conventional or separating zippers, the zipper is just that—centered—so that it looks exactly the same on both long sides when it is in place.

Because of the differences in the design of various garments, it's wise to follow the pattern guidesheet when you attach a zipper.

However, these general rules are useful for making a centered zipper application.

Stitch the seam below the zipper using a regular machine stitch.

Backstitch about ¼″ (6 mm) at the bottom of the zipper opening to secure it well.

- If the Centered Application is used for a separating zipper, skip this first step, since the zipper will open at the top *and* bottom edges.

Baste the section of the seam where the zipper will be placed using large machine stitches—about 6-8 per inch (every 25 mm)—and basting exactly on the seamline.

Press the seam allowances open.

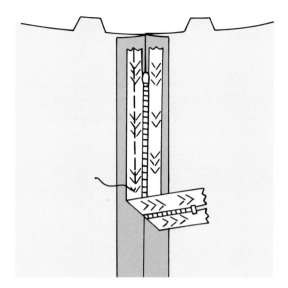

Place the right side of the zipper on the wrong side of the garment.

- The zipper teeth should rest exactly on top of the basted seam.

Baste or use self-adhesive basting tape to position the zipper accurately.

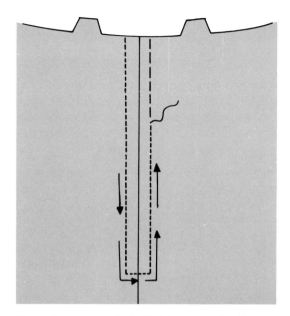

Place the garment, right side up, under the zipper foot.

Adjust the zipper foot so that your needle will stitch into the fabric about ¼″ (6 mm) from the basted seam.

Stitch, beginning at the top right side of the zipper, using a regular machine stitch.

Sew down the right side and pivot the fabric to sew across the bottom of the zipper about ¼″ (6 mm) below the zipper stop.

Pivot the fabric again and stitch up the left side of the zipper.

lapped zipper application

The Lapped Application is used for skirts or pants. The stitching is very close to one side of the zipper and a small lap is made to cover the zipper teeth.

Use a conventional zipper for most lapped applications. Separating zippers may be used in certain garments, such as ski jackets.

Stitch the seam below the zipper using a regular machine stitch.

Backstitch about ¼" (6 mm) at the bottom of the zipper opening.

- This step is not necessary if you use a separating zipper which will open at the top and bottom edges.

Decide which long side of the zipper will have the lap.

- In the side of any garment, the lap should be facing back.

- In the front of a girl's or woman's item, the lap should face left as the garment is worn; in the back, it should face right.

- Lapped zippers are seldom used in men's or boy's clothing but when they are, the lap on the front or back faces the opposite direction of the lap on women's clothes.

Press the seam allowances under ⅝" (15 mm).

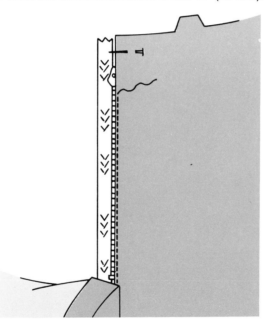

Place the closed zipper, facing up, under the folded edge which will not have a lap. The zipper teeth should rest next to the fold.

Baste or use self-adhesive basting tape to hold the zipper in place.

Edgestitch along the fold.

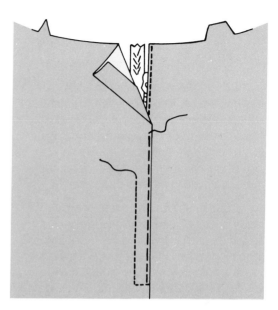

Baste or use self-adhesive basting tape to hold the lap in place so that it conceals the stitching you have just finished.

Stitch across the bottom of the zipper and up the side to form a lap.

- Stitching should be about ⅜" (10 mm) from the foldline.

fly front zipper application

The Fly Front Zipper Application is used in pants or skirts as a front closing. It is similar to the lapped zipper, but the lap is somewhat wider and the steps involved in sewing it are just a bit different. A fly front application can be made with a conventional zipper or a trouser zipper, available in notions departments.

Fly front closings can be completed in two ways, with the Mock Fly Front Zipper Application or the Standard Fly Front Zipper Application. When the garment is finished, both applications look quite similar but the Mock Fly Front is somewhat less complicated to make. It is often used for women's or children's clothes.

MOCK FLY FRONT ZIPPER APPLICATION

Stitch the seam below the zipper using a regular machine stitch.

Backstitch about ¼″ (6 mm) at the bottom of the zipper opening.

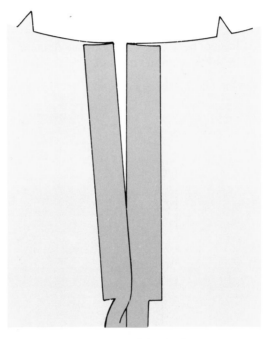

Press the extensions of the fly front under along the foldlines indicated on your pattern.

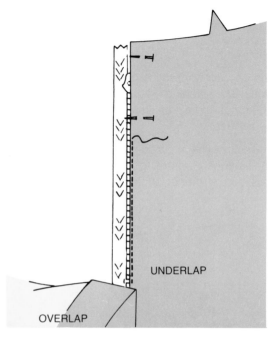

Place the closed zipper, facing up, under the folded edge which forms the underlap.

■ The fold should rest next to the zipper teeth.

Baste or use self-adhesive basting tape to keep the zipper in position as you sew.

Edgestitch along the fold.

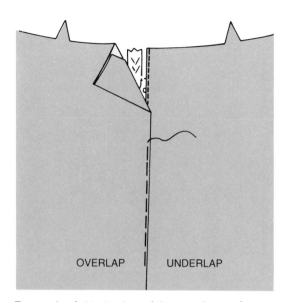

Baste the folded edge of the overlap to the zipper so that it conceals the stitching you just finished.

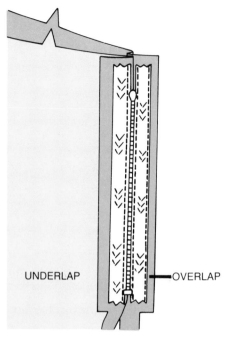

Place the zipper facing up so that the only sections under the zipper foot are the zipper tape and the seam allowance of the overlap.

Stitch the zipper tape to this seam allowance, sewing as close as possible to the zipper teeth.

Sew a second row of stitching about 1/8″ (3 mm) from the outer edge of the zipper tape.

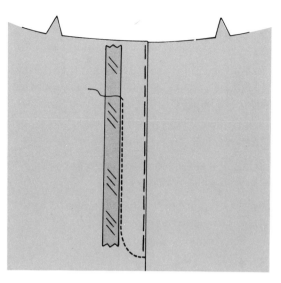

Stitch through all thicknesses of the garment from the right side, along the stitching line indicated on your pattern.

- To stitch accurately, place basting tape as a guide. Or, use hand basting or a paper guide to show you where to topstitch for a smooth, even fly front finish.

STANDARD FLY FRONT ZIPPER APPLICATION

To apply a zipper using the Standard Fly Front Technique, a small section of fabric is sewn to the underlap.

Follow these steps to make a Standard Fly Front closing.

Stitch the seam below the zipper opening using a regular machine stitch.

Backstitch about ¼" (6 mm) at the bottom of the zipper opening.

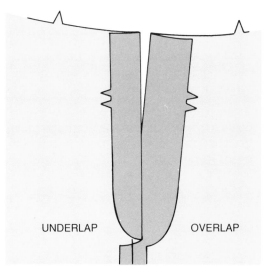

Turn the front extensions under and press the overlap along the center front line and the underlap along the foldline.

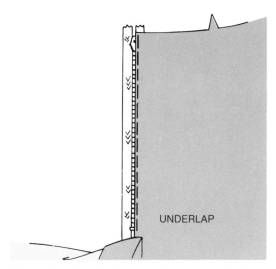

Place the closed zipper, facing up, under the folded edge of the underlap.

- The fold should rest next to the zipper teeth.

- Note that the top of the zipper will extend above the upper edge of the garment.

Baste or use self-adhesive basting tape to keep the zipper in position as you sew.

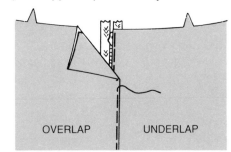

Place the folded edge of the overlap along the center front marking of the garment, to cover the zipper completely.

Baste by hand or machine through all thicknesses along the folded edge of the overlap to secure the area as you complete the opening.

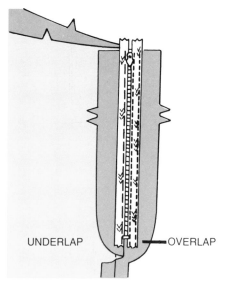

Turn the garment inside out.

Baste or use self-adhesive basting tape to attach the zipper tape to the overlap extension, keeping the garment free.

Place the zipper tape and the seam allowance of the overlap under the machine needle.

- Be certain that the garment is free so that no stitches will go through it as you complete the next step.

Stitch the zipper tape to the lap as close as possible to the teeth.

Stitch again ¼" (6 mm) away from the first row of stitching, closer to the edge of the seam allowance.

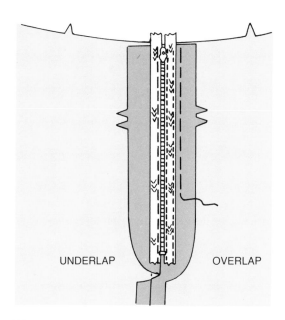

Place the garment flat so the extensions rest next to the outside layer of fabric.

Baste the overlap to the garment using hand or machine basting.

- Basting should be about ⅝″ (15mm) from the notched edge of the lap.

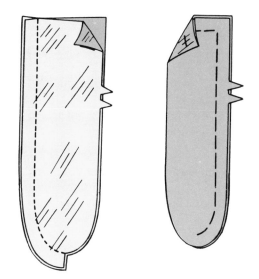

Stitch the fly lining to the fly along the unnotched curved edge.

Turn and press.

Baste the notched edges together.

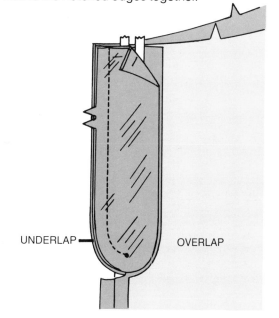

Pin the fly to the underlap, matching the notched edges.

Stitch from the top of the garment to the marking at the bottom of the fly.

- Be certain to stitch only through the fly and the extension, not the garment.

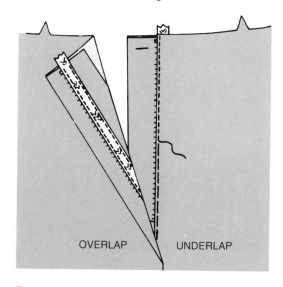

Remove the row of basting that holds the center front closed.

Open the zipper.

Turn garment right side out.

Stitch along the folded edge which rests next to the zipper teeth, on the underlap. Stitching should end at the bottom stop of the zipper.

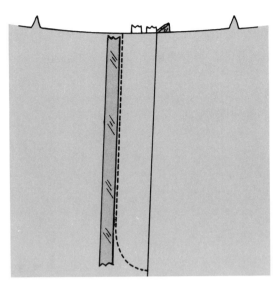

Mark the stitching line of the fly front on the outside of the garment, using a basting stitch or self-adhesive basting tape.

Topstitch through all thicknesses. Be careful to keep the fly free as you sew.

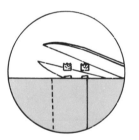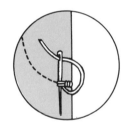

Trim the zipper tape even with the upper edge of the garment.

Reinforce the lower end of the fly front opening with a ¼" (6 mm) bartack.

- See Hand Sewing, page 77, for details about making a bartack.

invisible zipper application

This method requires an invisible zipper and a special invisible zipper foot attachment for your machine. Both items can be bought in a notions department.

When an invisible zipper is in place, it looks just like a plain seam. Invisible zippers are often used for dresses, jackets, tote bags and home decorating items, such as slipcovers.

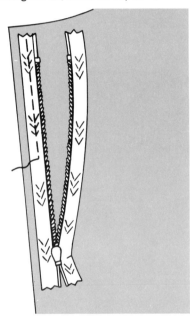

Open the zipper and place it face down on the right side of the fabric.

- The zipper coil on the *left* side of the zipper, as you are looking at it, should rest exactly on the seamline.

Baste, if necessary.

Adjust the invisible zipper foot so that the needle goes through the center hole.

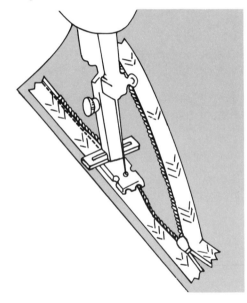

Roll the coil away from the zipper tape and place it in the inner tunnel of the invisible zipper foot.

Stitch along the zipper, through the tape and seam allowance, from the top to the bottom.

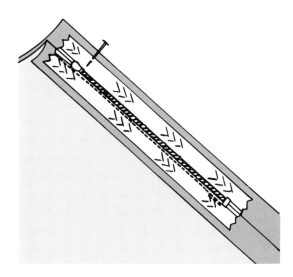

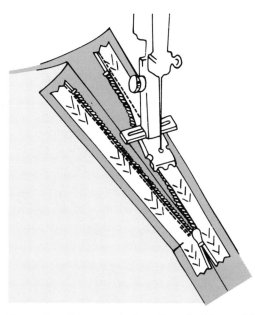

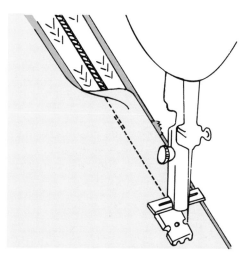

Close the zipper and position the coil so it is exactly on the seamline of the remaining fabric section.

- The zipper tapes will be resting on the seam allowances on the wrong side of the item.

Place a pin in the top corner of the unattached side.

- This will help you position the zipper correctly before stitching it to the other seam allowance. Do not remove the pin until you have the zipper ready to sew with the coil in position in the tunnel of the invisible zipper foot.

Open the zipper and place it so that the coil is on the seamline.

Baste, if necessary.

Roll the coil away from the tape and place it in the outer tunnel of the invisible zipper foot.

Stitch along the seamline next to the zipper coil, from top to bottom.

Close the zipper and slide the invisible zipper foot to the left so that the needle is in line with the inside edge of the zipper foot.

Stitch along the seamline, from the bottom of the zipper to the bottom edge of the garment, keeping the ends of the zipper tape free.

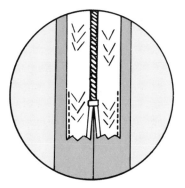

Stitch each end of the zipper tape to the seam allowances, holding the item you are sewing away from the machine so it is not caught in the stitching.

exposed application

This method is used in areas of garments or other items where there is no seam. It is very useful for knit fabrics or when a zipper is used for decoration.

Some separating zippers are attached with the Exposed Application. Follow your pattern guidesheet instructions to apply a separating zipper using this technique.

For conventional zippers, follow these general steps.

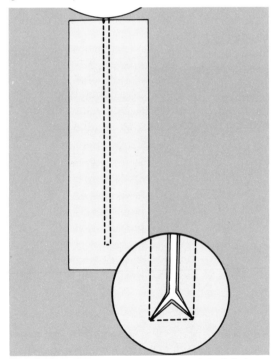

Cut a strip of firmly woven lightweight fabric, 3″ (75 mm) wide and 2″ (50 mm) longer than the zipper.

Place the strip on the garment, right sides together, over the zipper marking.

Stitch down each side and across the bottom of the zipper placement marking using about 14-16 stitches per inch (every 25 mm).

- The space between the two rows of stitching should be equal to the width of the zipper teeth.

Slash down the center and into the corners, clipping all the way to, but not through, the stitching.

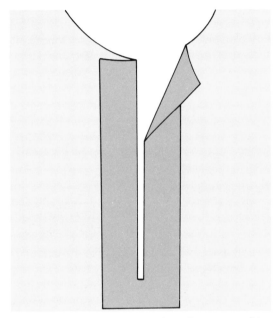

Flip the reinforcement patch to the wrong side and press, making sure none of the patch shows from the right side.

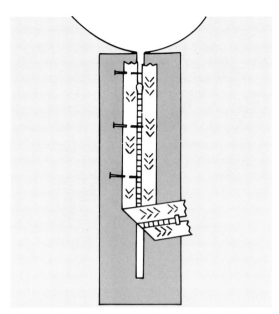

Center the zipper under the opening with the folded edges next to the zipper teeth.

Baste, if necessary.

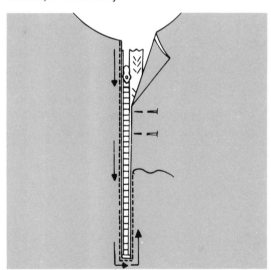

Edgestitch down one side, across the bottom, and up the other side of the zipper teeth.

careers that build on sewing skills

Did you know that you can put your sewing skills to work? It's true.

There are literally millions of men and women who have exciting, creative jobs which build on their sewing skills.

It's worth your while to investigate some of the interesting opportunities that rely on an understanding of textiles, fabrics, fashion design, promotion or sales and sewing techniques or equipment. Perhaps you'll find a job that's just right for you. Then you'll be able to plan ahead to develop the skills you need and get the special training or education that will make you a first-rate job candidate.

sewing: who needs it?

If you've never thought seriously about sewing as a career skill, it may come as a great surprise to realize how many of the things we all need must be sewn.

Just look around you. Who designed and made all the different clothes you, your friends or members of your family wear?

Even someone who sews plenty, can't sew everything that's necessary to live comfortably. For instance, who do you know who sews shoes? hats? handbags? umbrellas? gloves? bathing suits? football, baseball, basketball,

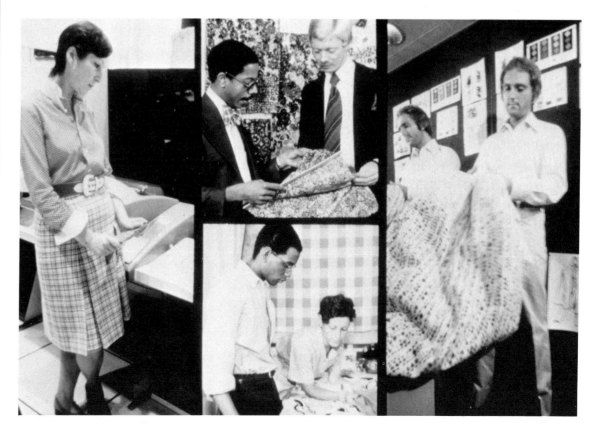

soccer or hockey uniforms? tuxedos? window shades? garment bags? suitcases? And what about the other everyday items we take for granted such as heavy-duty sacks for carrying mail, flags, typewriter covers, automobile upholstery, mattresses? Someone has to sew them.

Just imagine how many people are working so we can enjoy such an amazing assortment of clothes, sports equipment, home furnishings and other supplies.

So, who needs sewing? We all do.

thinking about a career

It's never too soon to start thinking about a career. Why not start today?

What is career? How much planning does it take? Isn't it just a matter of luck, after all?

A career is more than a job. In fact, *career* is the word used to describe the long-term work experience of a person.

A career could be one job, held for twenty, thirty, even forty or more years. Or, it could be a series of jobs, each with slightly different responsibilities and advantages.

Recent studies show that most people have as many as four or five jobs throughout their career. Of course, some people have many more.

Maybe you've already started your career. You might have a part-time job which will be the first step in a lifetime of work in a particular industry. For example, if you are working now as a salesperson or shipping clerk in a retail store, you might continue working there full time when you finish school.

Or, you might use the skills you've learned on your part-time job to continue your training and qualify for a more advanced position as a floor supervisor, assistant buyer, display specialist or advertising copywriter. The possibilities are endless.

But whether you have started your career or not, before you make one more career decision, think about what the world of work can offer you.

Remember, the average man or woman today works at least forty years after graduating from high school. That seems like a lifetime. It is.

Plan to make it an interesting, enjoyable one. You can do it. Many people do. It's the clever way to approach a career. Don't depend on luck to put you in the job that will offer a bright future.

Keep in mind that choosing a career is a commitment to yourself, your family and your community. The decisions you make about where to work and what to do will affect the way you and the people around you live.

the first step, analyze your interests

Begin thinking about your career by taking the time to analyze what you would enjoy about a job. Use the following questions as your guide. It might be helpful to write your answers to them on a separate piece of paper. That way, you'll have a handy summary of your interests and career goals as you compare job opportunities.

WORK ALONE, OR WITH OTHERS? HOW?

- would you prefer to work alone, or with other people?
- if you would rather work with others, would you enjoy working with elementary, junior high or high school students? with adults? with a special audience such as the handicapped or the elderly?
- would you like to be your own boss and set up an independent business? Or, would you rather work for a company and receive a steady salary?
- when it comes to getting a job done, would you rather take or give orders? Are you fair, but firm, in giving other people directions and helping them organize their work?

WORKING, WHERE? WHEN?

- do you want to work where you live now, or are you interested in moving to another place?
- would you like to work in a large city, a suburban or rural area, or perhaps in a foreign country?

- would you enjoy travelling on the job or prefer staying in one spot, such as an office, school, store or factory?
- does the idea of relocating as you advance in a company sound exciting? Or, would you want a job that would let you move ahead, right within your own community?
- are you willing to work irregular hours or on shifts at various times throughout the day? Or, instead, would it be most convenient if you could work a steady schedule, for example from 9:00 a.m. to 5:00 p.m.?

WHAT ARE YOUR SPECIAL TALENTS?

- how are your communication skills? Do you like to talk or listen? Write or read? Learn or teach?
- would you be comfortable in front of a large audience, on radio or television?
- do you have special technical talents such as the ability to repair machinery, type or use office equipment?
- are you artistic? Do you enjoy and have a talent for drawing or designing? Can you think up unusual and attractive ways to work with fabric or display garments?
- how's your fashion sense? Do you enjoy working with fashions to put together new ideas for wearing or accessorizing clothes? Would you like to help someone equip a home with handsome, comfortable and practical furniture, appliances or accessories?
- do you like comparing advertisements, displays or other types of consumer information materials to judge their appearance and effectiveness? Do you think you would enjoy developing projects which would alert people to new fashion trends?

DO YOU SEE YOURSELF SEWING ON THE JOB?

Careers in the textile, fabric and fashion industry range from jobs which require sewing to ones that depend on a general knowledge of what goes into making a garment or other item. How do you feel about sewing?

- would you prefer a job that allows you to sew or one that doesn't?
- if you did sew, would you rather work on detailed, delicate items such as creative accessories or large, specialized projects such as upholstery, draperies or awnings?
- are you clever at making alterations or repairs on garments to give them a new look or extend their wearability?

- would you enjoy the challenge of designing clothes for a particular audience such as infants, young children, the handicapped or the elderly?
- is industrial sewing your speed? Would you like the chance to work in a modern factory to make baseball mitts, hats, tennis shoes or other things?
- could you combine your interest in sewing with other interests? Costume designers, for example, blend their love of the theater with their knowledge of fabrics, design and garment construction.

Now, look over your answers. Have you identified a career that suits your future plans? Don't be too much in a hurry to settle on one

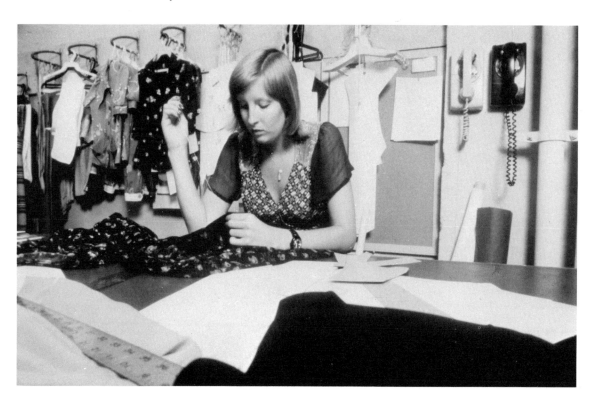

career choice. There's plenty more to learn about the many job opportunities that are available.

Just remember, no matter what your sewing skills or specialized interests, there are several employment possibilities that may be ideal for you.

careers in textile, fabric or fashion design

Designers are idea people. They have the unique ability to be inspired by art, nature, architecture, music, human behavior or many other influences to come up with exciting new methods for developing fibers, fabrics or fashion apparel and furnishings.

Most often designers work independently. They may work within a large company or completely on their own. But, in either case, the important part of their job is to do the research and sample making which results in something different, attractive and comfortable. It is a job that requires a great deal of concentration and self-confidence.

If you have a flair for color, patience to continue working until you have perfected an original thought and the practical sense to translate your idea into a useful item, designing may be your best career choice.

Designers need to be well educated in the basic technical skills of their profession. Maybe in the movies designing looks like it's just a matter of throwing fabric over a mannequin and inventing a far-out fashion with the wave of a hand. In real life, designing is a much more detailed and demanding experience.

A designer must know how fibers will work when woven or knitted into fabric, how fabrics will drape or tailor on the human body or on a piece of furniture and how fashions will adapt to the demands of daily living.

In short, a fashion designer must be an all-around expert on how people live and what they like to wear or use. That becomes obvious when you think about a specific item, such as a bathing suit or ski pants. A designer who makes them must understand the stresses and strains they will take and must be able to find fabric that looks good, feels comfortable and remains sturdy through many wearings.

Fashion might be foremost in many people's minds, but a designer must be equally concerned about wearability and durability.

Designers, of course, develop new ideas for just about everything you can name: shirts, sweaters, hosiery, dresses, tablecloths, bedspreads, sofas, sleeping bags, to mention a few.

Regardless of what area of designing interests you, the best experience you can have is designing and sewing clothes for yourself and friends. It will help you understand what fabrics work well for certain items and allow you to develop the judgment you will need in using certain sewing skills to achieve a particular design effect.

Part-time experience in selling fashions in a store is also valuable as you prepare for a designing career.

Just about every well-known designer has a degree in fashion design from a two-year or four-year college. These programs emphasize the details about buying fabrics wholesale, manufacturing, and other important aspects related to the creation and production of fashion items. You would be wise to enroll in such a program if you want to follow a career in the design field.

After graduation, most designers begin working as assistants to established designers. They may work for a large textile, fabric, pattern, garment or furnishings manufacturer. These starting positions may be highly competitive, so people who have on-the-job experience in retail sales plus a college degree have the advantage in qualifying for them.

The fashion capitals of America are New York, Los Angeles, Dallas, Miami and San Francisco. Internationally, the fashion capitals are Paris, London, Rome and Madrid. All of these cities, here and abroad, are stimulating centers for people interested in fashion and design.

Of course, there are small boutiques in just about every American city where people who want to remain close to their hometown can design and sell custom-made clothes or other items. But, to have a career in a major company or develop a national reputation as a designer, working in a large city is almost essential.

working as an illustrator or art director

Fashion is a changing style. New ideas and products must be presented to the public in an attractive, exciting way. Illustrators and art directors do just that.

If you have the talent for drawing or developing an imaginative new way to get across a fashion message, a career as an illustrator or art director might be ideal.

Illustrators are the people who actually prepare the sketches which show a garment, an item of furniture or a sewing skill, for example. Most often illustrators specialize in one type of drawing and generally focus their work on a limited range of products. Some illustrators prefer to do fashion art, others are best at doing technical drawings.

Turn back and look through the pages of this book. One person did the fashion drawings, another did the illustrations which detail the steps involved in sewing. Notice how each person has a particular talent for a distinct type of illustration.

Illustration involves more than inspiration. It requires a great deal of knowledge about how the human body moves and how fabric or fashions will drape or look in real life.

For instance, a person who works for a pattern company illustrating sewing directions has to understand exactly where and how every layer of fabric or stitch must be placed in a drawing. Otherwise a sketch which is planned to show a special technique would not be complete.

Fashion and technical illustrators spend a good deal of time learning sewing skills. It helps them as they draw illustrations which are attractive as well as realistic.

The best advice illustrators can give to people interested in this career field is to draw, draw, draw. If at all possible, enroll in a two-year or four-year college program which focuses on illustration. It will help you learn the facts about working with various art supplies and techniques to achieve the style you need to enter this creative area of the fashion world.

Art directors may or may not be illustrators. They are the people who take the sketches and place them in an interesting way on a brochure, advertisement, label or other consumer information item.

An art director must be able to select the appropriate size and style of type, decide how many illustrations are necessary for a project and develop an overall plan for how a finished book or other piece will look.

Again, look at this book. Why does it have three columns per page? Why is the type size convenient to read? Why are the fashion and technical illustrations placed where they are? Ask the art director. That's the person who made these important decisions.

Both illustrators or art directors may work independently, as consultants for many different projects sponsored by several companies. Or, they may work within one company as salaried employees who prepare the many projects of the corporation.

Within a pattern company, for example, illustrators and art directors work in many areas. Some work on the catalog, others on the educational materials, others on the guidesheets or pattern envelopes, still others on the annual reports or newsletters prepared for stockholders.

There are job openings for illustrators and art directors in just about every medium- and large-sized city in the country. Typically these professionals work for advertising or public relations companies, manufacturers, retailers or publishers. As a rule, the large cities, such as New York, Chicago, San Francisco, Los Angeles, Dallas, Houston, Philadelphia and Atlanta offer the most stimulating and varied number of employment opportunities.

A person interested in a career in fashion illustration or as an art director would be wise to begin working in these large cities, where starting positions are in abundance.

On the other hand, there are many local job opportunities for illustrators or art directors in small or medium-sized towns. Newspapers, department stores, and public relations or advertising agencies are excellent placed to start searching for a job in your community.

The clue to success is an attention to detail and a strong sense of responsibility in meeting deadlines. It's a challenging, creative field which will allow you to use your talents to their best advantage. Consider it as your career choice if you have an interest in art.

could you be an author or an editor?

What's the difference between an author and an editor?

To put it short and simple, authors write and editors approve or rearrange the writing as necessary to make the most of what has been written.

These are two closely related, but separate skills. Some people can do both things equally well, most people are better or more comfortable doing one or the other.

Are you a writer now? Many people enjoy writing, and it seems that a great number of them are interested in writing as a career. What does it take to make it as a professional writer?

To begin, you have to have a thorough knowledge of a subject. "A way with words" just isn't enough.

In the textile, fabric and fashion world there are many job opportunities for writers. They are needed to write sewing directions, care information, product facts, advertising copy and fashion fundamentals.

Just like illustrators, writers tend to specialize. Some have a very clean, sharp way of expressing technical details such as pattern directions. Others have a more loose, relaxed, even romantic, style in explaining new fashion happenings.

If you think you might enjoy writing as a career, start practicing now. Begin by reading. Read everything you can. What type of writing appeals to you? Once you decide, focus on that type and practice it until you become an expert.

Take writing courses, if you can. A four-year college degree is an excellent foundation for a career as a writer. Besides your journalism or creative-writing courses, choose a major that will give you something solid to write about. For example, if you are interested in sewing or fashion, a major in Home Economics with a specialization in Clothing and Textiles would be your best bet.

Writers must have a great deal of self-discipline. They cannot wait around for "inspiration" but must be able to accept and deliver an assignment on schedule.

Equally important, writers must develop objectivity so they can accept constructive criticism and change their copy, as necessary, to suit the requirements of a client.

Editors also must rely heavily on objectivity. Building on the same basic journalism training as writers, editors must also have the ability to think in broad terms. They must be able to explain to a writer exactly what ideas must be included in a chapter or article. They have to be able to edit or cut out unnecessary sentences or thoughts and rearrange paragraphs or sections to make the final piece a crisp, thorough one.

Both authors and editors can work independently or with a company. They are in great demand by publishers, manufacturers and retailers concerned with sewing or fashion.

Many of the job openings are centered in large cities, particularly New York, Chicago, San Francisco and Philadelphia. However, there are exciting opportunities in just about any city. Newspapers, public relations or advertising agencies, department stores and many other local businesses are always in the market for good writers and editors. You'll probably be able to find a job in this career field, right where you're living now.

Be prepared for a beginning job. Learn to type. First of all, very few professional authors ever submit handwritten work. In fact, most major publishers of magazines, brochures or books would not accept it. Further, many of the entry-level postions as assistant copywriters or editorial associates require typing. It is not at all demeaning to type on the job. Instead, it is the most basic skill of a career in writing or editing.

other careers in communication

Writing, of course, is an important method of communicating, but even if it isn't your major talent there are many interesting jobs in the fashion industry that may be just right for you.

Public speaking or education are two main areas that rely more on being able to communicate by word of mouth.

Would you enjoy appearing on radio or television? Would you like to teach a class of young people or adults? Why not? It's exciting and challenging.

Just about every major fabric, pattern or fashion company hires travelling representatives. These people attend conventions or visit department stores and other places to explain the latest information about a product.

It's a job that's as demanding as it is rewarding. A person who enjoys travelling and is able to handle the responsibilities of meeting deadlines, dealing with unexpected delays or changes and speaking with the public would be an ideal candidate.

The best training for a job as a travelling representative would be experience as a salesperson, teacher or performer. In other words, any activities that would help you learn to be comfortable in dealing with consumers, either individually or in a group, would be useful in preparing for a career as a travelling representative.

A four-year college degree in Home Economics with a major in Communications, Journalism or Radio and Television is essential for most entry level positions in this field.

A travelling representative does not have to be unusually good-looking but certainly must be attractive, well groomed and able to speak clearly and effectively to many types of audiences.

Many people believe that travelling on the job is a fantastic experience. It can be but it can also be lonely or difficult. The most successful travelling representatives are one who are able to enjoy being alone, almost as much as they enjoy being with other people. Remember, if you travel as part of your job you will probably spend at least a good deal of time on your own as you move from place to place.

Some people who travel set up an apartment near the center of the section of the country they serve. That way they can return home on weekends or during times when their travel schedule is light. Other people are required to spend several days or weeks each month at company headquarters so they have apartments in a large city such as New York, San Francisco, Chicago or Atlanta, near the corporate offices.

For someone who's interested in a travelling career, it's a good idea to travel as often as possible as a student. It gives you the opportunity to learn firsthand what it means to buy airplane tickets, check into hotels and otherwise handle the requirements of getting around.

Of course, people who plan to travel on the job should be able to drive an automobile and enjoy flying.

It's also important to recognize that travelling representatives work irregular hours. One day is never like another. Sometimes you may have to meet with an audience at 8:00 a.m., other times you may be working until midnight.

This variety is the spice of life to many travelling representatives. They truly prefer working at unusual times and in many different places. Perhaps you will too. Or, is education a career field that interests you? It is also an important area which depends on the ability to communicate.

A sewing teacher, for example, must be able to explain exactly how and why a special skill is necessary. Think about the way you learned to sew. Who taught you? Could you do as good a job teaching someone else? If so, consider a career in education.

is selling your special skill?

There are positions as salespersons at every level of responsibility in the fashion industry. You could sell thread at a local store or sell millions of bolts of fabric to a major manufacturer.

Both jobs are equally satisfying and both require the same basic skill, to recognize what product will do the best job and help a person make the best buy. In either case, a complete knowledge of sewing is essential.

People who sell must be sensitive. They must understand the needs of other people and be able to make recommendations which satisfy the customer. In other words, a salesperson is in the business of giving good advice.

If you like working with people, enjoy comparing the advantages of various products and like to share your expertise with others, you may be cut out for a career in selling.

Would you like to try your hand at it? That's simple enough. Get a part- or full-time job at a local retail store. There are many openings which will allow you to learn the business from the beginning.

Eventually you may decide on selling as a career. Then you can enroll in an occupational Home Economics program at the high school level or a two-year or four-year college level program after graduation. If you decide on college, select a major in Retailing in Home Economics or Business Administration.

When you do, don't just concentrate on the classroom. Although this is a well-known aspect of the education field, you may be interested to learn that there are as many job opportunities outside a classroom as inside one.

For example, did you know that community service programs such as Day Care, Adult Education or Senior Citizen centers employ teachers? They do. So do department stores, fabric boutiques and many other places within your hometown and in just about every other small or large city across the country.

Teachers must have a thorough knowledge of their subject, but just as important, they need an open reassuring personality to help people progress at an individual rate. Any teacher will tell you, that's not always easy. Patience is a prime quality that any teacher must develop.

If the field of education appeals to you, investigate the opportunities in your area. Make a list of all the schools or community centers which employ people to teach sewing or fashion facts. Be certain to include Extension clubs, 4-H, Y-Teens, Scout groups, training programs for the handicapped and all of the other services that help others learn sewing skills. You'll be amazed at the length of your list.

To prepare for a career as a teacher, enroll in a four-year college program with a major in Home Economics and an emphasis on Education as well as Clothing and Textiles.

You can enter the sales field either on the buying or selling side. You might be an assistant buyer who helps select the merchandise which is offered for sale. Or, you might be a sales supervisor who coordinates the work of many other salespeople and helps to train them to do a good job.

Buying and selling may be a high-pressure business. In some cases, you will be paid a commission on what you sell. Then your very income depends on how effective you are. For example, many interior designers who help

people select furniture, draperies or other major items receive a percentage of the sale as their salary. People who enjoy selling say this is stimulating and encourages them to work efficiently. You ought to know if you would welcome this incentive before you enter a sales job which bases your salary on the amount you sell.

Did you know that the average department or chain store is open more than 70 hours each week? It is. That enables people who work as salespeople to arrange their schedules more or less at their own convenience. You can work during the morning, midday or evening hours. You may even be able to work on certain days of the week, as you prefer. Many salespeople see this as an extra advantage.

Perhaps the most exciting aspect of a sales career is flexibility. Who buys the buttons that are on all the jackets in a department store? A buyer for a major manufacturer. Who sells the drapery hooks or curtain rods to the interior designers in your community? A salesperson for the manufacturer of drapery supplies.

You can start a career in sales just about anywhere, selling just about any product. Then when you are ready to advance, you can move on to working for a manufacturer or retailer to buy or sell in volume.

The skill of selling or buying is a specialized one. If you think you would enjoy it, get some good experience in the fabric, pattern or fashion departments of your favorite store. There's no better way to prepare for your future.

the many careers in manufacturing

Manufacturing is an industry which offers jobs for people with a talent for working with machinery.

You could be a cutter, who uses heavy-duty power equipment to cut out many garments or layers of fabric at one time. You could be a bundler, a person who sorts the various pieces which belong to one garment and delivers them in sets to a sewing machine operator. Or, you could be a supervisor or inspector who checks the accuracy or efficiency of the completed work. There are also many job opportunities for mechanics who know how to repair or maintain the intricate equipment involved in cutting, sewing, pressing, packing or shipping fashion items.

Manufacturing was, at one time, a very difficult job which required workers to sit or stand for many hours in crowded, noisy factories. Today, fortunately, manufacturing is a highly specialized career field with many well-planned, ventilated and lighted work areas.

Mills or manufacturing plants tend to be centralized in certain sections of the country. Upholstered furniture is made in North Carolina and the surrounding states. Garments are made in the Northeast, throughout New York, New Jersey and Pennsylvania. Hosiery, carpets and items such as towels, sheets and blankets are generally manufactured in South Carolina, Georgia and nearby areas.

If you live in a manufacturing center you probably already know people who work in mills. Ask them about their jobs and write letters to the major companies which employ people to help manufacture things. You can learn a great deal about the opportunities available.

Most positions in manufacturing require a high school education, However, a degree from a two-year college with a major in Heavy Machinery repair or Industrial Sewing would be a distinct advantage in qualifying for a starting job.

People who work in a manufacturing plant often begin assisting on the assembly line. That is, they might help carry fabric pieces to the sewing machines or hang completed garments on hangers. Advancement is rapid for people who are eager and interested in learning specific skills. For example, a person who specilizes in sewing zippers or sleeves can soon take over as a sewing machine operator.

other ways to put your sewing skills to work

You may like to sew but not want to accept a full-time position sewing.

Why not invent your own sewing specialty and make a career for yourself?

Dressmaking or making alterations is one excellent example. You can place notices in local papers, on shopping mall bulletin boards or in other prominent places. Offer to do the big and little sewing jobs that other people can't complete.

You might, for instance, specialize in adjusting hemlines, sewing on buttons for a laundry, or restyling children's clothes to make them last for one more season. Be specific as you advertise. Tell what you can and cannot do. Be polite and punctual as you get your work done. Before you know it, you'll have a whole range of clients who will come to you first for sewing assistance.

This is an especially versatile way to begin a career. Many young parents find it an ideal opportunity to combine the responsibilities of raising children with the challenge of building their own business.

Here are just a few possibilities: making draperies, sewing slipcovers, appliquéing decorative aprons, pillows or other items by hand or machine, smocking children's dresses, creating interesting accessories for a boutique. No doubt you'll think of many more ways to accent your sewing skills as you create your own small company.

Many states have created special vocational programs for high school students to train them in the latest speed sewing equipment and techniques. These schools may even offer courses in computer technology and inventory control, which are important aspects of modern manufacturing methods.

Some vocational programs also offer on-the-job training or counseling to help a person decide which area of manufacturing offers the most potential in planning a career. You should be aware that the graduates of these vocational programs are in great demand so if you have your mind set on a career in manufacturing, enroll in a vocational program as soon as you can.

If you prefer, you can work for a department store as a tailor or an alterations expert. You'll enjoy regular hours and, of course, a regular salary. You'll also be responsible for doing a great variety of sewing. One day you may have to hem a coat, another day you may have to add some width to the side seams of a playsuit. There's one thing for certain, every day will be interesting.

On the other hand, you might want to become an expert at sewing one type of product. Who do you think sews awnings? Or banners? Or embroiders evening gowns? Each of these unique talents must be done by a person who has a complete understanding of sewing and the ability to adapt the specialized requirements of a design to complete a project.

These jobs may be done as an independent worker or as an employee of a company. Look around your neighborhood. No doubt you'll find people sewing where you never recognized them before.

Will sewing become more than a pleasant pastime for you? It could. In fact, perhaps it should. Like millions of other men and women, you could build a career on your sewing skills. Just think about it.

index

Y

Z

#1